D1504455

SURVIVORS OF WWII IN THE PACIFIC

Ronny Herman de Jong

SURVIVORS OF WWII IN THE PACIFIC

Ronny Herman de Jong

* * * * *

Formatting and cover design by Debora Lewis
arenapublishing.org

Cover photo courtesy of Canstock

ISBN-13: 978-1500746414
ISBN-10: 150074641X

Luctor et Emergo

CONTENTS

INTRODUCTION

The year was 1995. September 2, 1995 to be exact. I stood on the deck of the USS Missouri, the "Mighty Mo", anchored in the harbor of Bremerton, WA, on the actual spot where, in 1945, the Japanese Contingent signed the Instrument of Surrender together with representatives of the Allied countries that had participated in World War II in the Pacific.

That all-important date, September 2, 1945, when the end of the war and the Japanese surrender became official through a document signed and dated on the deck of the USS Missouri anchored in Tokyo Bay, went by me completely for many years. What counted for *me* as the end of the war was August 15, 1945, the day my parents hung out the flag every year and celebrated.

My first book, *In the Shadow of the Sun*, based on my mother's secret camp journal, was published in Canada in 1992, so from her and through research I knew a lot about the war and the dire circumstances of women and children in camps on Japanese-occupied Java. But it was not until 1995, when I was invited to the 50th commemoration of the signing of the official surrender document and stood on deck of the USS Missouri that I realized the immense significance of that moment, fifty years ago. I walked over to the bow where three 16" gun barrels pointed straight ahead and wept. My family had survived. I owed my life and my freedom to countless men and women who had fought the bloody war and won.

Ever since that day, I have given more thought to not only other camp survivors, but to the young men who went to war, not fully realizing the horrors that were in store for them, the young men who, if they survived, are now aged veterans. Through their stories I have learned a lot more about the War in the Pacific.

And so, three years after I published my second book *Rising from the Shadow of the Sun: A Story of Love, Survival and Joy*, and after I heard the stories of those camp survivors and veterans I had the privilege to meet, I decided to write down those stories about people who deserve to be remembered; stories that, if they are not recorded, might be lost to the rest of the world.

The stories sound alike; the pain and suffering, the tortures and killings are similar. The lucky ones survived and were able to talk about it eventually, for future generations to know what the destruction of war can do to human beings. And then again, sometimes their experiences were so painful that they prefer to relate funny incidents instead. One of their survival skills was their sense of humor.

I am eternally grateful to all veterans who fought in that "Deadliest Conflict in Human History", to all who fought in wars that followed and those who are still fighting for the freedom of our country. May there be peace on earth one day, with nothing but abounding joy and love.

Ronny Herman de Jong, Author, *Rising from the Shadow of the Sun: A Story of Love, Survival and Joy.*

VERA RADÓ

A Teenage Prisoner of the Japanese

Vera Radó, living in the Blue Mountains of Australia, emailed me to get a copy of my second book. After reading it we became friends through shared camp experiences and similar interests. Vera is an amazing survivor. At the moment Vera is enjoying life and taking ballroom dancing lessons. She sent me her unpublished Memoir, written in 1995.

It's August 1995, and I am sufficiently far removed from the traumas I suffered as a teenage prisoner of the Japanese more than fifty years ago to tell about my experiences.

The process of rehabilitation and healing I went through can be visualized as a very long, stony, winding, uphill path, full of obstacles over which I kept tripping, stumbling and falling, only to scramble up and limp on–at times too depressed and despairing to want to continue. But at times also buoyed up by an understanding, caring remark.

I have made that weary journey, and I have reached the top, and, although nothing will ever erase the memories, deeply etched as they are within me–within all of us who were part of it–I can now walk reasonably erect and even with a measure of stability. Pain and distress will never fail to strike me again and again at recalling this period of my life, but the all-consuming terror, the continual feeling of crisis, the anxiety, have left me. I am in calmer waters now and almost daily find myself thanking that universal force of which I am a tiny fraction for steering me safely through the tempests of my earlier life, and I can share my Memoir.

When the Japanese forces attacked Pearl Harbor in December 1941 I was fifteen years old and lived with my family, consisting of my mother, father and brother Ivan, in Surabaya on the island of Java, in the former Dutch East Indies–now Indonesia. Surabaya was the Dutch naval base, and consequently, became a target for Japanese air raids. They started in early February 1942, and the first one, aimed directly at the heart of the city, caused many deaths and a lot of damage.

By this time there were air raid shelters built in most private backyards and also in public places, and soon, with sirens wailing often twice a day, we were spending more time in the shelters than anywhere else. It was an anxious time, spent listening to the hum of the bombers, the whistle and thud of falling bombs, and wondering whether we were going to survive yet another day. School was suspended and soon all outdoor activity, such as swimming, playing tennis, etc. ceased.

Halfway through February came the shocking news that Singapore had fallen, and my mother urged my father to pack up and leave. But he could not be persuaded. Broadcasts remained optimistic–to boost morale–even when the Japanese marched through Sumatra, beating back every resistance, and then landed on the shores of Java. By then it was too late to flee. Within a matter of days the Japanese Imperial Army came marching into Surabaya.

It was a black day, that 8th of March 1942, in more than one sense. The oil tanks on the southwestern edge of the city were being blown up by the Dutch to prevent the precious fuel from falling into enemy hands. From early morning there was a huge pall of smoke hanging over the city, and against this ominous backdrop we watched the occupying army's progress through our street. First we saw tanks with the red-on-white flags flying, then trucks and armored cars, then masses of soldiers on foot and on bicycles. They looked triumphant, but we were trembling with apprehension at what was in store for us, whilst peeking through the louvers of our locked front door.

Immediately after the occupation we had to register at the Town Hall and obtain identity cards, which we had to carry on us all the time and show on demand. Whenever we met Japanese military personnel in the street, we had to stop and bow deeply. If we were on our bikes, we had to step off, and bow – or risk having our bikes confiscated. Cars, including doctors', were requisitioned, radios had to be handed in to be sealed, so that only the local stations could be received. Very soon all public servants were rounded up and imprisoned – from the Governor General down to the most junior clerk. This included all male teachers. So school ceased altogether. Some school buildings were used as POW camps, and some continued with native teachers teaching native children. Whenever I passed my old school I could near the kids singing "Asia Raya", the song of Free Asia, and there were posters everywhere proclaiming "Asia for the Asians". The Japanese were out to extinguish all European influence in Asia, and establish their own 'Greater South East Asia Co-Prosperity Sphere' with Japan as supreme leader. It was part of their ideal to establish Japan as the dominant power in our part of the world and to eradicate all white colonialism. To be replaced by Japanese colonialism one presumes!

A women's camp was set up in one of the suburbs of Surabaya, called the "Darmo Camp". It held about 6000 women whose husbands had been interned, and their children. The gates finally closed on them in January 1943. My father, along with a small number of other Europeans who worked in essential industries and services, was still needed, so we were still free. The Japanese had no army doctors with them, so they imposed on my father and about a dozen other physicians at all times of the day, mostly to treat them for venereal diseases. However, as the last of the white population was clapped into prison, our turn came too.

Doomsday arrived on 31st August 1943, the Dutch queen's birthday. My brother and I had to go to Council Chambers in the morning on official business, and when we returned at lunchtime, my father had already been taken away by Japanese soldiers. They had ordered my mother to pack for herself and us and be ready to be interned in a couple of hours. The time lapse had given my Mum a spell to figure out what to pack, and to this day I have to praise her for her presence of mind. I watched her as she pulled out the bottom drawer of her dressing table, and upended it into her suitcase. It was full of patent medicines. By this act of foresight she saved my life–and that of a few others.

Presently, the Japanese returned, and we were taken by 'dokkar' (horse-drawn carriage) to Werfstraat Jail, a regular jail for criminals, murderers, thieves and what-have-you, which also served to house political prisoners. At the gate we had to say goodbye to Ivan, who was led away to the men's section. We joined a queue of women and children, amongst whom we recognized friends and acquaintances. We were registered, stripped of money and jewelry, and led away in small groups.

The compound to which we were taken was surrounded by high stone walls topped with broken glass. There were six large cells with barred doors and big copper padlocks. Each cell was meant for ten to twelve persons, but we were pushed into them with about forty women and children. At the back of the cell was a hole in one corner for a squat-toilet, and there were mats on the stone floor for us to sleep on. At 6 p.m. the doors were banged shut, and with the sharp click of the key in the padlock we were left in no doubt as to our status. We were prisoners of the Japanese. For how long?

None of us slept much that night on the cold stone floor. The noise of children crying and mothers shouting and wailing was like something out of a nightmare. The mothers were deeply traumatized, and the children inconsolable. All they wanted was to "go-o-o h-o-o-me"! There was no privacy at all, so when someone had to use the toilet, we stood with two or three together as a shield in front of her. The single toilet soon became a source of continuing stench. In the morning we were let out for a bath in a nearby block, and it was a relief to be able to move around and get away from the ruckus. We were mixed in with Iraqi women and children, whose standards of hygiene were not quite the same as ours. After a week, at our request, our group of about one hundred European women and children was moved to another part of the jail. It had a more pleasant aspect – for a jail, that is. It even boasted a few trees. There were two rows of ten one-person cells, separated by a cyclone fence with open gate, two bathrooms in a separate block opposite the cells, and the whole of it was enclosed by high walls of rough woven bamboo reinforced by barbed wire. We called it "The Paradise".

At this stage of our prison life we had enough to eat. The food was cooked in the prison kitchen and was meant for mainly native prisoners. There was an unchanging menu of boiled rice, vegetable soup, tofu, a bit of chili paste and occasionally a banana for each. The vegetables were never cleaned; they were just thrown into the pot roots and all, and the bottom of the food drum always contained a layer of sand, bits of string, wire, and–sometimes–a cockroach or other unidentifiable bit of protein.

The most distressing part of our jail existence was the witnessing of the torture of political prisoners, sometimes by sight, but mostly by sound. Opposite our enclosure was a row of small cells. Men were taken daily from there to another part of the jail back of our compound. We could clearly hear the bellowing of the Japanese and the men's terrible screams. One man kept shouting for his mother. After the interrogation, having been beaten unconscious, the men were taken away on a stretcher and thrown back into their cells. We could not escape this horror. It went on incessantly and relentlessly.

Once, we saw over the top of our wall, a man being tortured on the upper gallery of the administration building opposite us. This poor unfortunate had his wrists tied behind his back, and had been hoisted up by his hands until he stood on tiptoe. A Japanese soldier was barking at him, stabbing him repeatedly with a burning cigarette. I quickly turned away my eyes, but the picture will always remain with me. At another time, a woman who had been locked up in a dark cell in solitary confinement for some weeks, was released into our section and promptly committed suicide by hanging herself in her cell. It was left to her young son to cut her loose. These events unnerved us all.

In March 1944 we were ordered to pack, loaded onto a long train the following morning and moved to the other end of Java, to a small town called Tangerang, 20 km west of Batavia (Jakarta). The train journey, which normally would have taken twelve hours, took three days in a train with all windows and doors locked and all blinds down, and with no provision for food or water.

On the second day, at our request, as all of us, but especially the children, were limp with thirst, we stopped for water from a railway siding pump (for filling up the steam trains) and promptly got the runs. Our carriage was packed with bodies; we sat on the floors and in the aisles. The seats were for the elderly. The single toilet soon over-flowed, and thereafter became a disaster area, defying all description.

On the third night we arrived at a dismal looking dimly lit station, and had to walk for almost an hour to our destination. The smaller children had to be carried, as they were too exhausted to walk. We finally reached a large building behind a massive bamboo-and-wire fence with four watchtowers, one on each corner. Although there was some food ready for us to eat, all most of us were capable of doing was to find a place to stretch out and sleep. I have never slept so soundly on a hard wooden board!

We found out later that our new 'home' was a former corrective institution for delinquent youths. We also discovered that we had been traveling with about 1500 other women and children from the "Darmo Camp" in Surabaya plus the contingent of about 100 Iraqi women and children from whom we had been separated earlier in Werfstraat Jail.

Tangerang Camp consisted of large wards built around two courtyards with a central kitchen, flanked by four rows of single cells (meant for the worst offenders?). The wards had wooden boards two meters wide, running along both sides in two tiers, one at a height of one meter, the other above that at about two meters from the floor, with a ladder in each corner to climb to the 'top floor'. My mother and I found room at the top; the climb up the ladder was definitely worth the airier aspect of the upper story.

Here we lived for a year on hard work and diminishing food rations. Our daily meal consisted of one ladleful of glutinous sago porridge in the morning and a 5 cm wide piece of bread made of unleavened corn flour. Half of this piece was meant for our evening meal. At midday we received one cup of boiled rice and one scoop of watery vegetables, in which our 'meat' ration was also cooked. With a bit of luck we at times found one or two small cubes of meat - mostly tripe - floating in the brew on our individual plates. The Japanese got incensed if we complained about the small rations, and told us we should be grateful for what we got, as food was in short supply. They themselves looked well-fed.

Soon, every second person contracted malaria, and all of us had at least one bout of dysentery. I got both diseases, but -thanks to my mother's foresight in packing quinine-at least the malaria could be controlled. The dysentery kept recurring all through my imprisonment, and to this day I am suffering from the damage to my digestive system. My mother had an extremely painful episode with a kidney stone, for which there was no painkiller strong enough in her medicine kit. Fortunately, she passed the stone after a few days and was put on light kitchen duties, cleaning the vegetables grown by our "garden team" of which I was a part.

The worst experiences in this camp were the periodic visits by the supreme commander over all camps in Western Java, Captain Sonei. This individual was a lunatic - in the true sense of the word. He was reputed to go out of his mind at full moon. We were notified of his visits the day before, and ordered to have everything looking neat and tidy.

On the day of his arrival we had to line up on the tenko field where daily roll call was held. As Sonei entered with his interpreter, we received a command "Kiutske!" (stand at attention), while he climbed the dais. At the command "Kèrèh!" we bowed deeply to acknowledge his supremacy over us, miserable wretches, then came "Norèh!" (at ease), after which he would shout, rant and rave at us for about an hour, pausing at times for the interpreter to translate in Malay. His speech was always the same–we owed deep gratitude to his divine emperor's great bounty in providing us with food and a roof over our heads. Any complaints or breaches of the rules would be severely punished.

Then came the moment we were all dreading. Sonei would pause, sweep us with a malevolent glare, and pick out someone at random from our ranks, gesturing for the woman to come forward and stand in front of him. This poor, defenseless victim would then be beaten senseless with open hands and fists, until she fell to the ground, when she was given a few hefty kicks with his boots. "And this," Sonei would say with a nasty smirk, pointing to the bleeding body at his feet, "is your example. This is what happens to those who disobey the rules."

One of his victims died of internal injuries. After the war Sonei was tried by the Dutch for war crimes and hanged. He professed not to understand why he received such harsh punishment, since he was only doing his duty for his emperor.

One year after our arrival at Tangerang, we were put on a transport again, this time to Camp Adek in Batavia, where we joined about 4500 other women and children from that region. Although this concentration camp was larger than Tangerang, room was at a premium. We were packed into the wards like sardines; each individual got 55 cm of space. By this time we had all been whittled down in size by poor nutrition and sickness, but 55 cm is a tiny space for living, sleeping and eating. There was, of course, never a lack of border disputes–sometimes very loud ones. Tempers were easily aroused, as everyone was under stress, hungry and irritable. Women who were responsible for small children, in particular, were under almost unbearable pressure to keep themselves and their offspring alive.

Rumors kept flying around of great successes by the Allies and of impending liberation, but nobody had a radio. The regular house searches had seen to that, so we did not know what was really happening. In fact, we were completely cut off and isolated from the outside world. The rumors actually kept us going, because by this time–mid-1945–we were nearing the end of our endurance. Many of the very old and the very young had died, and even young girls of my age group were getting ill and dying with increasing frequency.

14

There was a small team of women in our camp, detailed to build coffins—made of woven and split bamboo—for burying the dead, and they were kept increasingly busy. By this time the death rate had risen to four to five persons per day. Most of us had lapsed into a state of apathy, consistent with long-term starvation. I myself found that I no longer very much cared whether I was going to die in this wretched camp or be liberated. We were all dreaming of food. It became a major preoccupation with many, even an obsession, resulting in the incessant exchange of recipes for one or the other divine dish.

We were also beginning to disbelieve the rumors of Allied victories. So far they had been proven false. Maybe the Japanese were winning, and maybe we would all soon be dead. I certainly felt that I would not last another six months. At nineteen, I was minus energy, suffering from chronic diarrhea, the beginning of beri-beri, and incapable of any great physical effort such as digging gardens and growing vegetables, which had been my previous task. I was given permission to resign and rest in the garden under trees, adjacent to the tenko field.

Then, suddenly, in mid-August, we were getting more food—an extra leg of beef, more vegetables from the markets, even a small fish each. Oh, the smell of it! We couldn't believe it at first, then started to suspect that something important had happened. It was not until mid-September 1945 that we received orders to assemble at the tenko field, and were told that the war was over. Just that, no explanation, no further information, except that we were also told we could leave the camp 'at our own risk'. We soon found out why. Two women who left for their home in the city were ambushed by rioting young Indonesians and murdered.

It's a miracle we survived–not only the years of imprisonment but the aftermath of the Japanese occupation. There was a full-scale revolution going on in Java, where the Japanese had for years brain-washed the younger generations of Indonesians to throw off the colonial yoke. The rampaging Indonesian youths (pemudas) imprisoned the Japanese, whom they had come to view as detested occupiers, then turned on us, hated colonials. They murdered a sizable number of former civilian prisoners, including women and children, before the British troops finally landed on Java and evacuated us to Singapore. Not too many people know about our plight during this political vacuum, yet it is part of World War II history.

My mother and I were eventually reunited with my father and Ivan in Surabaya. By then the city had become a cauldron of seething fanaticism and hatred. We barely escaped being attacked and butchered as we were taken to the harbor in a convoy of trucks with a Ghurka soldier positioned on the roof of each one, machine-gun ready. We traveled between thick rows of angry natives, hissing at us and looking very threatening. It was a great relief to embark on a British landing craft and watch Surabaya disappear in the distance.

We had been totally at the mercy of the Japanese occupiers, then again at the mercy of the rioting Indonesians. It was a wonderful relief to arrive in Singapore, even though we landed in another camp. But this was very different. We were free, we were well-fed, and–above all–we were safe!

We learned later that the atomic bombs had ended the war. It killed many Japanese civilians, men, women and Children, but it also saved hundreds of thousands of lives of prisoners of the Japanese, like us. Violence, death and destruction are inevitable in wars, but we have to take a balanced view, because all sides suffer casualties. In the end, nobody wins.

An extraordinary childhood and unexpected education opportunities in later life led Vera Radó to make her bequest to the University. Vera grew up in Java, and between the ages of 17 and 19 was imprisoned by the invading Japanese in World War II.

After being evacuated to Singapore by the British, she spent three years in The Netherlands catching up on lost schooling. After graduating from high school, she returned to her parents in Surabaya, Indonesia, and in 1950 migrated to Australia, where today she lives in the Blue Mountains.

Inspired to further her education in Australia, Vera enrolled in a Bachelor of Arts with a major in Philosophy at Macquarie in 1980, and graduated in 1989.

Explaining her interest in philosophy, she says: "It was a lifelong ambition, going back to childhood, to find answers to the fundamental questions in life."

"I was the sort of kid who pestered her parents about the whys and wherefores of everything. During my internment I also learned the harshest lessons of my life, including facing my own death, which gave me an added impetus to study and widen my outlook."

Vera chose Macquarie University for its flexible curriculum, which meant she could combine philosophy studies with other relevant subjects, such as semantics (vital to logical reasoning), and ancient Greek and Latin (used by early philosophers).

She put her degree to good use by teaching at Sydney U3A (University of the Third Age) from 1993 to 2000, mostly in subjects such as social philosophy and the philosophies of politics and religion.

Vera cites having had the good fortune to study during the years in which university fees were abolished by the Whitlam Government as a key factor in her being able to achieve her education ambitions. Conscious that some students are unable fulfill their own education goals because of their financial situation, she was motivated to make a bequest to the University.

"Having neither descendants nor financial obligations, I decided to show my deep appreciation for the opportunity given to me to study under the finest lecturers in one of the best tertiary establishments in Australia."

These included Dr Luciana O'Dwyer who taught Vera about phenomenology, and Edmund Husserl, now one of her favorite philosophers; Dr Ruqaiya Hasan, who fascinated her students with lively talks on semantics; Emeritus Professor Max Deutscher (philosophy); Tony Palma (Greek philosophers); David Blair (linguistics) and Vic Dudman (logic).

Vera's aim is to benefit future young students, and as part of her bequest has made a stipulation for an annual scholarship to be awarded in philosophy and the humanities.

Vera had a part in a short promotional film which features John Misto talking about his award winning play THE SHOE-HORN SONATA.

WALTER HOBÉ:

Memories of the Japanese concentration camps as experienced by a young boy, War: 1942-1945

I met Walter Hobé in 1995 on the deck of the USS Missouri in Bremerton Harbor, Washington. For him, the commemoration of the signing of the Instrument of Surrender, to which we had been invited, was an even more emotional event than it was for me: being five years older than I, he still had vivid memories of the camps. We remained friends through the years, across the miles. Walter lives in Canada with his wife of over 50 years, children and grandchildren. For his eightieth birthday, he wrote his memoir, for family and close friends only. Excerpts are below.

I was born in April 1933 in Yogyakarta and later moved to Batavia. My time in Japanese prison camps had tremendous impacts on me, physically, emotionally and spiritually, which I have had to live with the rest of my life. Those memories, coupled with Japan's on-going insistence on ignoring this period in history, have kept the issue of restitution a constant undercurrent in my life.

The period in my life up to 1941 was marvelous. We were healthy and happy. Those were the years I remember as being heaven on earth. Beautiful, lush country; wonderful people of a variety you will not find anywhere else. It is a country that can be considered one of the most densely populated in the world.

The Japanese had invaded Korea and the Chinese mainland on July 7th, 1937, of which we children were blissfully unaware. But Sunday, December 7th, 1941 stands out in my memory. We did not go to church that Sunday morning because of devastating world news. We had an old Philips radio in the corner of the dining room. My parents were listening to the radio broadcast from Honolulu and crying their eyes out. The Japanese were attacking Pearl Harbor. My father said, "How long will it be before they come here?" Little did we know that at the same time they had attacked Hong Kong and Malaya.

The Dutch government declared war on Japan the next day. However, there were Japanese "sleepers" living in the Dutch East Indies who had immigrated there years before; highly trained officers of the Japanese Imperial Army. Everything had been betrayed. Even the re-organization of government was already set up, so that when the Japanese forces came in, the new government could take over the next day. Our bicycle repairman turned out to be a Japanese officer and our barber was seen riding a white stallion wearing his officer's uniform, giving instructions in Dutch to his prisoners.

I remember the day the Dutch Government decided to destroy all their holdings so that they did not fall into the wrong hands. I was sitting in the cherry tree in the garden, looking out over the horizon. There was no sun. It was very eerie. Thick black clouds were hanging over the city with a terrible stench of sulfur in the air. All the oil installations in the harbor had been set ablaze. The day had turned into night. The perpetrators were later hanged by the Japanese.

At the beginning of the war, when my father was out of work, he started a little business. He went to the market on a bicycle and bought bags of flour and peanuts. Since life had sort of stopped–stores were still open but you could not get to them–my father started baking bread for the neighbors. The metal basins that we used to do the washing in were standing in the yard, covered with tea towels. Underneath, the dough was rising in the sun. We had little pans made so that we could make small loaves of bread from the scraps of dough on the side. Quite exciting for us kids! Father also made peanut butter. Or rather, we did. The meat grinder was modified with a special blade and we would grind the peanuts to pulp. After putting the pulp in a jar, we had to stamp it with the palm of our hand to make it go down. Well, when you fill a Mason jar with peanut butter, after stamping it you will find only half the jar is peanut butter and the other half is oil. The oil was siphoned off and used for baking, and the jars were topped off with more peanut butter. Sometimes we also put *sambal oelek (hot chili paste)* in the peanut butter–delicious! We sold this and it was such a success that, after my father was taken prisoner, we continued the business with the help of our *djongos (male servant),* Timan.

On 14 Jun 1942 my father got arrested. He was taken away by truck. We followed on our bikes but could not keep up. Later we heard that he was brought to Adek. The next day the Japs came and stole our car, which was hidden in the garage. Somebody in the neighborhood had been talking...

On October 2nd, 1942, my mother, brother and I were transported to the Kramat Prison camp. Kramat was a busy thoroughfare through Batavia with big, statuesque properties. The house that was assigned to us had a very large veranda with four heavy pillars, and a huge garden in front and back. On the side was another building which formerly housed the staff. We had a big room on the side of the staff building with a door to the outside. The three of us were very comfortable there. Our big armoire divided the room into two so that my mother had some privacy. My brother and I were sleeping behind it. Just outside the garden to the front was a wall of bamboo matting and barbed wire, to prevent us from going out, and also to prevent people from coming in, because the poor natives would have liked to walk away with most of our possessions.

In March 1943, the prison camp was closed. We could not get out any more to do business with Timan. However, he kept watch. There was a guard at the entrance to the camp, a Japanese soldier with rifle and bayonet. The Japs taught us that we were very low people and that we had to bow down even to the common soldier. We soon found out what that meant–when we did not bow down deep enough we were in for a beating. I once saw a very tall, good-looking, proud Dutch lady passing a guard and nodding in his direction. She was called back and had to stand at attention. An officer was summoned, the situation was explained, and he went at her. But since Japanese men are usually of small stature, this officer had to jump in order to hit her in the face. He saw the silliness of the situation and grabbed his sword from the sheath and started to beat her over the head. It did not take long for this lady to fall on her knees, all bloodied and bruised. He was satisfied and let her go. I was only 9 years old–my first experience with brutality.

Two streets down a 9-year-old boy got meningitis and died. That made quite an impression on me. Little did I know that I would also get that disease at age 22. Once there was a lot of commotion outside camp Kramat. We peaked over the wall and saw the *kampong* (native village) across from our camp on fire. This was a big disaster as the houses were made of *bilik* (bamboo) with *atap* (palm leaf) roofs. There was no fire brigade as we know it; there was no water to douse the flames. So everybody ran in all directions to save their lives.

On Aug 29th, 1942, at a moment's notice, we (2,500 people) were told to pack our belongings and stand ready at the gate for transportation to somewhere. That was the Jap's favorite pastime. With a bamboo stick in his hands he herded us on: hurry, hurry, hurry! Whatever furniture we still had had to be left behind. We could take only our mattresses and our trunks. We were taken to Tjideng Prison Camp.

Later on in Tjideng, we got a moment's notice to get everything out on the street We had to stand at attention, ready for inspection. Again we had to stand in the hot sun for hours. A uniformed guy on a motorcycle arrived, wearing a black *topi* (hat) like the Indonesians. It was Sukarno as head of the police, working for the Japs. He stopped and looked at our stuff. Various things were taken away, and we had to move on and leave things behind. We had to go to the other side of the camp and move in with other people.

Then we had to be counted. We would *kiotski* (stand at attention) in three rows of ten, facing towards Japan and the

Emperor, and count: *ichi, ni, san, si, go,* etc. There was one person in charge and he had to report to the Jap that all was well *(ijo arimassen,* everything in order). We had to bow down *(keirei)* and stay that way till the Jap was satisfied we did it well enough and then dismissed us *(naore).* Of course, it was under the blazing sun! Sometimes it took minutes and sometimes hours, depending on their mood.

When we heard Japanese speak to each other, the language sounded stunted and rough, like a grunt. And when they raised their voices they sounded like animals. We were scared of them! We never talked back, because it always had consequences. When we spoke to them, it had to be done in Malay. If they found out that you understood Japanese you were automatically considered to be the go-between, and when anything went wrong you would get the first beating.

Tjideng was just on the other side of town. My mother had to work in the hospital, so it was our task to move our things. To this end we obtained the bottom of a baby carriage. We fastened a plank to it and thus we were ambulant with our trunks and mattresses. We also did some work. Some gardens still had grass and this had to be cut. Since it was very hot, we only walked around in shorts. We conserved our energy and our resources by washing as little as we could. The laundry was done with a little water and soap, if there was any, and then we left it on the lawn to be bleached by the sun.

School was not allowed. However, there was a small area on the side of the house shielded from the front by a wall, where a lady volunteered to teach us. We wrote on a slate, as there was no paper. Needless to say, these were not accredited courses, so that after the war, I was missing four years of primary schooling.

These were scary times, because the freedom fighters outside the camp would jump over the walls into our prison camp and steal the clothing off the wash line, and whatever else they could gather. Our boys and girls had to stand watch at night. To that end, they were armed with bamboo sticks. They could never catch these *rampokkers* because they were naked and had covered themselves with soft soap.

In the prison camps there were no Bibles permitted, unless they were approved by the Japanese. My mother had taken a whole set of handwritten sermons from her father when she moved to the Far East. When church services were not allowed anymore, these sermons were circulated until they fell apart. If my grandfather only had known that his sermons would serve a dual purpose!

Each day we were fed three meals. Well, meals...the vegetables were the leftovers of the Japs; sometimes we only got the green carrot tops. We got meat... mostly it was only animal bowels and stomachs; we had to clean them before cooking. We volunteered our services in the camp kitchen in order to be in line for scraps. "Give us this day our daily rations" we prayed jokingly.

The older women had to work in the park. Formerly a sports park, it now had to be dug up by hand in order to grow sweet potatoes (*ubi*) for the Japs. When harvested and kept out too long, these potatoes became *bongkreng* (rotten) and then they were fed to us. To this day I hate them.

The normal daily food intake was 80 grams of uncooked rice, some vegetables in "bowel" soup with Spanish peppers, 100 grams of tapioca or cassava gruel, and every five days a five centimeter long piece of tapioca bread, which was very hard and rubber-like. In order to eat it you had to soak it in water and every day you ate a slice. Children got half that ration. Children under five and people over 60 were the best candidates to die. Tjideng camp was quite big with more than 10,000 people. A one-family home now housed 50 people. It was not easy to keep the peace among each other. There was a "person in charge" (*kepalla*) in each household, selected by the occupants. This was quite an honor that had to be earned. When the Japs came into the house, this was the person they addressed, and when everything was not satisfactory, this person would get the beating. The kepalla was also in charge of the counting. Twice a day, we had to gather on the street in front of the house and stand at attention in rows and count down: *ichi, ni, san, si, go, ruku,* etc.

Tojo (40th Prime Minister of Japan and General of the Imperial Japanese Army) said, "NO WORK, NO FOOD." So everybody was working. We had to dig some big holes and build toilets over these. These latrines were placed everywhere in the camp. They were called the "palaces". The lady in charge of the palace was called "the palace watch". The more the war progressed, the more malnutrition took its toll. One of the symptoms was chronic diarrhea. It was therefore absolutely necessary to have these palaces close by, so you could reach them in time of need. The pits of these palaces filled up quickly, and were open. You can imagine the smell. Sometimes the contents were used as fertilizer.

There were continuing razzias. People still had too much *barang (stuff)*, so one day all the stamp collections had to be brought on to the field where the Japs burned them. There were still dogs in the camp. A truck covered with planking was brought in and we had to collect all dogs and kill them. To that end we grabbed them, strung them up with rope and beat them with a baseball bat, till they were dead. This was all for the entertainment of the Japs. This happened just a week before we were put on a transport to Tjimahi (August 22, 1944).

Our camp commander was Sonei. During full moon he would go crazy. He would enter the camp at night and would slash around with his sword. Anything in its path would be cut down. Days before he was already unbearable; even the Japanese guards were afraid.

In the yard behind the fence there were mango trees, but the mangoes were guarded extensively by their owners. We invented a contraption: a long bamboo pole with a little bag on the end, and scissors with a spring on a rope. Over the fence, without anybody noticing it, we gathered fruit. Of course we could not wait till it was ripe...stomach aches galore! But that did not deter us, as long as we had something in our stomach. Then there was the *jambu* tree, with *jambu ayer* (mountain apple). Everything in season, naturally. There was this lady who had a rooster and asked us to kill it for her. Yes, we needed a knife. Two guys held the rooster while one cut his neck. The rooster started running and we could not hold him. He ran into a brick wall and made a crack in it. Little did we know that this rooster was used for cockfights–he was very big and very strong. We were also experts in killing pigeons. We were not allowed to have them any more, because they might be used for communication outside the camp. In the end, there were no more animals to be slaughtered as we ate them all. Except for the forbidden fruit... the two monkeys in the cage belonging to the Japs!

All this time we did not know where my father was. On August 29, 1944, my brother was taken away and I was all alone. Then the time came that I also had to leave. The Japs feared that when boys were big enough they could cause trouble with the girls. Yeah right! Through malnutrition our hormones were not working, although our minds were going and we talked a lot, like "he is going with her" (smirk, smirk). I was dressed in my best *packiejan* (suit) and taken to the gateway. After saying our good byes, we had to line up outside the camp to be counted, and then jump into a truck.

It was February 25th, 1945. The last thing I saw was my mother crying at the camp entrance. Five hundred boys were put on that transport. As it turned out we were driven to Mangarai train station, where we had to hop over the tracks to a passenger train standing far off. Now it was almost dark; the windows were closed so that we could not see out. Was this done for our protection? This train was always used for the natives, and we called it class *kambing* (cattle cars). There were three rows of benches, two on the sides and one in the middle. Natives always traveled with their animals to market, chickens, ducks, geese or goats. The trip lasted the whole night. Stop and go, stop and go. No water, no food. It was getting colder, so we knew we were going into the mountains. In the morning we arrived at our destination, Tjimahi Prison Camp.

After getting off the train we had to assemble in order to be counted. It looked like we were in the middle of nowhere. To our right we saw a big building that turned out to be the military hospital. We were marched up the highway towards our right. If we had gone left we would have been going towards Bandung and to the 4th Battalion prison camp where my uncle and my brother were, but I did not know this at the time.

We passed an arch that said Baros 5, another prison camp. On our right, we passed a police station, headquarters of the *Kempetai*, the Japanese version of the KGB or the FBI. Finally, to our right, we entered an arched gate and we saw a street with houses on both sides. It was part of a pre-war military camp with a smithy and horse stalls. We marched to the end of the street and were assigned a house. It was totally empty. We were introduced to two adults. They were to be our *kepalas* (housefathers). "Where do we sleep?" "On the floor." I had my little suitcase and used some clothing for a pillow. I also had my flannel black-and-white striped army blanket. So now we had to find the softest spot on the floor. We felt each tile, and in the corner the tiles were "softer" so that is where I found my spot.

Then I really got a problem—I cowered in my corner sick with longing for home. I could not eat or drink. The housefather watched me and talked to me, but it didn't help. After about a week they took me to a doctor who told me in no uncertain terms that I had to grow up fast, take a hold of myself, otherwise he would give me one week to die. It took me another couple of days to get up and leave the house.

In front of the house was a *slokan* (gutter) with running water from a spring somewhere. To my surprise, there were small fishes in it. I built a little dam and started to catch them. Afterwards, I dried them in the sun and had a little extra protein with my rice. The bathroom had a big *mandibak* (water tank), common in all houses. Standing on the side, I could look from the bathroom window over the fence and see the *sawahs* beyond. In my mind, this was the picture of freedom, and I vowed that one day I would walk in these *sawahs* towards that mountain in the distance barefoot, so that I would feel the mud in between my toes. I did not realize that behind the mountain was the cemetery Leuwigadja where all my compatriots were buried.

We did not stay there very long. We had to cross the highway to the other side of the camp. House 37b was assigned to me with 27 other boys. Now we could sleep on wooden benches lined up on both sides of the wall. So in every room there were two benches, sleeping about ten kids each. We had a back yard which was walled in. We dug up the yard and planted tomatoes and salad. This was quite secure, as nobody but the occupants of the house could get there. This way we could get a few extra vitamins. Still, you had to guard your tomatoes, as sometimes it happened that one day they were green and the next day they were gone! I was not sick a single day, so maybe it was good for something. We did have chronic diarrhea though.

We all were dressed alike. The clothing that I brought with me I never wore. The only thing I wore was a *tjawet* (loincloth) provided by the Japs. This was very handy going to the bathroom. We had no toilet in the house. Fortunately, because we were in the mountains, a mountain stream ran through the camp. We sat on the embankment and did our business. There were always a bunch of us together. We made it a habit to observe each other's stool. As soon as blood was detected in the stool, we had to go to the doctor. I had to report the boy sitting next to me to the doctor, as he would not go himself. He had dysentery and died a week later. It was necessary to observe the strictest hygiene, so we often washed our hands. One time we were sitting on the side of the stream when somebody noticed a water snake coming towards him. En masse, we fell backwards into the water, grabbed it, skinned and cooked it, and ate it.

We sometimes had fun, too. This stream ran further into the camp, and at one point they had made toilets over the water (mostly for the older people, so they had a little privacy). They would squat over a slit in the floor. We were outside, upstream in the water. We waited till all the cubicles were filled and people were squatting...then we put a piece of paper on the water and lighted it with a match. When it floated underneath them, they all got burned and jumped up, holding their private parts. This all to the great merriment of us kids!

The older people had to work outside the camp on a farm. On this farm, there were animals, like cows and pigs. They were for the *Kempetai.* Next to the farm was the cemetery Leuwigadja. I never went there. Every morning we had to carry a whole bunch of dead bodies out of the camp to join the bodies from the other prison camps. Sometimes there were more than 100 a day. We carried them in bamboo crates. These were not too well constructed and sometimes would fall apart in transport. Because of the condition the bodies were in, and because of the tropics, the bodies would sometimes fall apart as well; a leg or arm would fall out of a crate. It was a somber sight every morning. The military hospital close to the station was now moved to our prison camp across the street, in the houses

33

that we first occupied. That is where I found my uncle Piet, suffering from *beriberi* (edema).

We were inventive and thought of a way to smuggle money for food. We boys had to work as well. All hands were needed. We had to haul wood for the kitchen fires. Therefore, we joined the elders pulling wagons to the train station, loaded the wood and came back. Next to the station was a park. When we needed to relieve ourselves we had to ask the guard. But behind the bushes natives were waiting, which was prearranged, with foodstuff. We were naked except for a loincloth, and we were wearing *klèteks* (wooden slippers). We had gotten money, which we put in Aspirin tubes up our rectum. When we "relieved" ourselves we retrieved the money and obtained pieces of meat cut in strips. These were put in a little bag that we carried between our legs. Upon returning to the camp we had to go through inspection. They never grabbed us between the legs, so we always passed. The wagons with wood were offloaded under scrutiny, so we could not hide anything in the wood. The meat was not for our consumption, though. It was cooked and fed to the sick in the hospital. One little cube of meat a week would cause the beriberi to slink. My uncle did not make it. He died the last day of the war.

We all suffered from lice. To that end, we were shaved bald so that the sun would kill them. One day there was a transport of sick people from the other camps to our hospital. Walking there among the carriers we could ask them questions, whether they knew of this person or that one. I found somebody who was looking for me–it was my brother! Apparently we had passed each other a couple of times without recognizing each other. He had grown tall, was dressed and wearing glasses. I had remained small, was naked and bald. From him I learned that my other Uncle Jan was also in that camp and that my father was in the 10th Battalion in Bandung. That was the only time we saw each other during that period–just for half an hour! The next time some people were sent on transport to Bandung, we made sure that they had messages for family members. That way my father also got to know where I was.

This was our daily diet: our mornings started with *toebroek* (black coffee). It was still dark then, and cold. We would be sitting there shivering in our blanket, *djongkok* (hunched), sipping the coffee. Breakfast came, made of tapioca starch, and if you did not eat it right away, it separated into water and sludge. Lunch was a roll, baked in my brother's camp. The yeast was a Dutch invention. A chemist had found out that urine had a good source of Vitamin-B. To that end, there were big drums set up in the prison camp into which everybody had to pee. These drums were brought to the kitchen and boiled. The rotten stuff separated and the yeast remained. The bread was baked, but the rolls were hard.

Dinner consisted of a cupped hand of boiled rice. Sometimes there was little "meat" in it, usually of bowels and tripe. Vegetables were usually discarded by the Japs (now, we would call them inedible). Since the Japs had the habit of punishing us for whatever, we had to prepare ourselves for eventualities. From the bread, I sliced off one slice and dried that in the sun. The next day, I ate it as if it was toasted, and sliced off two slices. In a week, I had saved myself another roll. The same I did with the rice. Every day I saved a spoon of rice and dried it in the sun. The next day I would add water and eat it, saving two spoons. Boy, did that come in handy when our camp was punished and we did not get food for two days! The first day, I said, "Ah ha, I am smart." But the second day, I was smarting. I never have had so much pain in my life from an empty stomach. At this time I was so thin, that when I inhaled and held my tummy in, I could feel my spine from the inside. I could completely cover my shoulder blade with my hand. When I moved my bowels, I moved them all right-at least 15 cm of bowel was hanging out, which I had to pull in before finishing. At this stage of the war, the natives were perhaps even worse off than we were. There was a gutter around the camp through which we crept to get close to the natives. We agreed that at a certain time we would be there with clothing and they had to provide food (*gedekken* it was called-smuggle). I bartered most of the clothing that I still had for bananas. A *sisir* (comb) of little milky *pisang soesoe* (sweet bananas) caused my diarrhea to stop immediately for ever.

Our house was situated next to the hospital exit. We heard a commotion outside one day and we went across to the hospital to check it out. What had happened? A native farm laborer with a spade on his shoulder had sauntered passed the Japanese guard. When the guard did not pay attention, he hit the guard over the head with his spade. The guard went down and the native ran away. However, the sentry at the main entrance had watched the proceeding and sounded the alarm. The native was caught and brought to the main entrance. There he was tied up with a rope slung over a beam, his hands tied behind his back, lifting him up so that he was standing on his tip toes. As soon as he got somewhat comfortable, the rope was pulled up. In the end, his arms were stretched out above him but they were wrong side into the socket. The guard wanted to interrogate him, and hit him over the head with the same spade. The handle eventually stuck in his skull and he died. We were watching this from afar, horrified.

One time, the Japs came in unexpectedly and forced some chaps to bring their table outside. They were just having lunch, so it was the hottest part of the day. They were forced to run around the table in the sun, until they collapsed. Another time, some guys were rounded up. They had to stand opposite each other and had to slap each other in the face. At first, they figured out that when the one's hand "hit" the other's face, the other would clap with his free hands–as long as it made the sound. But then the Jap got his sword and started to participate. Well, that stopped that in a hurry! In no time at all, two best friends were now hitting each other as hard as they could, because it was a matter of survival.

When I went to a reunion in Holland after the war, I met a colleague of mine from KLM. I found out that he had been in the same prison camp as I. When I reminded him of this incident the said, "Why do you think my eye is crooked?" We had made friends with the guys that were working in the kitchen. These were enormous, tall and strong guys. I was very small. Anyway, one day one said, "Come and visit me and play with my cat." He had finished the night shift and had heard a cat's meow outside the camp. Well, he made a hole in the wall and caught this animal with a basket. It was ugly, with pus in his eye, and he had no tail. The next day we came again and wanted to play with this cat. "He is in the bathroom," he said. In the bathroom was no cat but only a pail. "No, look above and behind the door!" A skinned cat hung behind the door, and his pelt was in the pail. We cooked it-they had the meat and we had the soup.

One day, a huge Liberator bomber flew over the camp. I climbed on top of the roof as it was circling the camp. Suddenly, the bomb bays opened and boxes were thrown out hanging on parachutes, like manna from heaven. They appeared to be Red Cross parcels. These parcels contained, among other things, cans with sweet milk, chocolate, cigarettes, etc. We could not eat the chocolate-the bars were too hard. The instructions were to scrape off little pieces and put them in boiling water. Thus we had chocolate milk. Otherwise, it was too rich for our bowels and we could die. But it was a beautiful experience to see these airplanes drop their goodies. It reminded everyone of the manna from heaven. Years later I was waiting on the ferry to go from Truro to Prince Edward Island. I got to talking to the guy in front of me and he asked me where I was from. I told him Indonesia. He knew it well, he said, as he had been flying as a navigator in Liberator bombers, dropping parcels in the camps. Needless to say, there were no dry eyes there.

As was the custom, we had to congregate three times a day to be counted. This one time I remember as if it was yesterday. After all the formalities, the Japanese camp commander gave a speech. He told us the war was over. This was about September 22nd, 1945. Everybody joined in singing the National Anthem *Wilhelmus*. To this day, I get tears in my eyes when I hear it, reminding me of this day. I climbed on the back of one of the kitchen helpers and cried, "Now I can go back to my Mamma!" The adults had already known what was coming. It appeared that there was one radio in the camp all these years. It had not been discovered.

Then came the day that somebody warned me there was a strange guy waiting for me at home. I rushed home and met this guy, who claimed to be my father. He had come from Bandung to pick me up. "Well, I am sorry, but I do not know you and I am not going with you." He said that he had already gone to the 4th Battalion Prison camp and picked up my brother who was waiting outside behind a tree. We took my scanty belongings and I had to get dressed. The clothes still fitted me somewhat. Now we had to report to the front office. My father identified himself to our Dutch camp commander and I was released into his custody. Outside the camp, my brother appeared from behind the tree. The three of us now started walking, but we had no strength to carry the stuff and go any distance. My father had no money to hire a native's transportation. Fortunately, we heard a Japanese truck coming our way. We stopped it and hitched a ride to Bandung. We were now reunited with our father, and a new chapter in our lives had begun.

When we arrived in Bandung, we settled in into a big hangar type building. My father had occupied a corner and had built two additional beds of bamboo for us. That was the only building material we had. The bamboo is hollow. It can hide all kinds of creepy crawlers... so we were bitten at night. There was a sweet smell around the bed: bed-bugs! Well, out with the bed, into the sunshine, and stamp the legs and beat the bedding! One night, I slept with my mouth open and when I woke up I closed it, crushing a bed bug which had settled on a molar. It smelled like cilantro, which I cannot eat to this day.

This 10th Battalion camp was huge. It housed many people from all kinds of back-grounds. A lot of inventions were done in the camp. A lighter for instance. Mostly made of a piece of steel against a flint rock with some dried moss it was made by an engineer, of course. It was a copper cylinder with a wooden head. You took the cylinder apart and put dry moss into it, then closed it and hit it hard with your hand. Due to the compression, the moss would burn and you could light a cigarette or a paper with it. Another invention was the water pump. It was made with hardly any tools of all kinds of scraps. They were able to sink a pipe, with a filter at the end, some 100 meters down. We had very clean drinking water there. Talking about cigarettes, my first smoke was a rolled up dried leaf of the corn husk and my tobacco was the hair. Well, this was a coughing ceremony if you ever saw one. And with my history of bronchitis, this was my lesson never to try to inhale anything but clean air.

Now that "peace" had come, we were all upbeat, with lots of expectations for the future. It is a feeling that is hard to describe. We were going to rebuild, learn from our mistakes and make a better world. The first thing to do was to regain our strength. My father had some money and we went outside the camp to the local market. We bought a little chick and a big chicken. The big one was for immediate consumption, the small one was to play with. We let that little one roam around our beds eating the bed bugs. In no time, this became a big chicken and...

This was the only time we went outside to market. We were told that things had changed and it was too dangerous. We could now no more trust the Indonesians. A boy, slightly older than I, was caught at that same market in view of the camp. He was tied to a tree and *chinchang*-ed (killed with knives). We could not do a thing. The Japs did not do a thing either, although Lord Mountbatten had told them that they were responsible for our well being. These soldiers were short of cash and were selling their weapons to the *pemudas*. A couple of days later a bunch of these *pemudas* were trying to shoot their way into the camp. We had to hide as the bullets were flying around us. They did not succeed.

There were already transports of POWs going to Batavia. An acquaintance was going, and my father asked him to take a pair of wooden sandals he had made for my mother. We had engraved them by burning her name on it with a magnifying glass. To this day I have these slippers as a memento. My mother did not wear them out.

My father had the opportunity to have himself declared unfit for work by a doctor, who recommended us to recuperate in Australia. The Red Cross saw to it that we would meet our mother at the departure point. We were put on a train transport to Batavia under heavy Gurkha guard. We now had some protection from the British Gurkhas. The Indonesians had a holy respect for these Gurkhas as they were bald with one little string of hair. They were slit-eyed and fiery. With a sten gun in their right hand and a curved sword in their left, they were unbeatable. We arrived safely in Batavia where trucks were waiting to take us to a hotel. The hotel was completely sandbagged and we slept on the floor. Again, we were arguing which was the softest tile. This was necessary, as it does not feel nice to have your protruding bones making contact with something hard. At night, however, we could not sleep. We came from the mountains and were used to cool weather. Here, the air was so thick and hot that you could cut it. Outside, a fierce battle was being fought with machine guns and hand grenades.

The next morning, we were loaded in trucks and driven to Tandjong Priok. On arrival at the quay, we saw a crowd of women standing there, eagerly staring up to the trucks. My brother cried suddenly, "I see her!" The truck had not come to a standstill yet, but we jumped out. We did not need to worry about luggage-we did not have anything, not even a toothbrush. (We brushed our teeth with crushed brick and our fingers) My mother was very thin and wearing our slippers. After our embraces and crying, we looked at each other and felt like strangers. My father had not seen my mother for three and a half years. For us it was a little shorter, but it seemed like a lifetime. I was now 12 years old and completely independent. After all I had been through, I was an adult. I had not been sick one day, except for some ulcerated wounds. If you punctured your skin, infections would start and they became big, round, open festering wounds. There was no medication, so we tried drying them in the sun. But the most difficult thing was to keep the flies off. The best thing to do was to put your leg into the river where little fishes would eat away the pus-very painful, though! These ulcers would eat away the skin. My brother was less fortunate. He had no more skin on most of his lower leg. It was now all bandaged. After the war, we got medicine, a yellow powder, that was freely sprinkled on the wounds and the skin would grow back after a while. Unfortunately, on part of his shin the flesh was completely gone (this eventually would cause his demise). The skin did not could grow back, and he always wore a bandage over it.

At Tandjong Priok we boarded a Japanese freighter, a miserable looking ship which took us outside the harbor to a big ocean liner, the MS *Oranje*, a hospital ship, on which we sailed to Australia and a new adventure.

Hannie Blaauw
Camp Stories

Hannie Blaauw is a very special friend. I met him about ten years ago when I moved to Arizona. Born and raised on Java, he is eleven years older than I, so he was a teenager during the years of Japanese oppression. He survived the camps and vividly remembers the cruelties he witnessed. He was always hungry. He had camp sores and tropical diseases like all of us, but he survived thanks to his sense of humor and his guardian angel who protected him many times in harrowing situations.

Born in Tegal, Central Java, Hannie had five brothers. His father died before the war. When the Japanese occupied the island, the family was separated; his mother was sent to a women's camp, his brother Adriaan, who had an education as a nurse in the army, was put to work in a camp hospital in Bandung to treat Japanese soldiers. He was part of a medical team of military doctors and nurses. They were not transported overseas, the Japs kept them on Java to treat wounded or sick Japanese soldiers. Brother Eddy was shipped to Thailand to work on the Burma railroad. Brother Albert was sent to Japan to work in the coal mines. Hannie, his oldest and younger brother were incarcerated in camp Tjimahi together. His oldest brother would die in Camp Tjimahi.

Food was scarce. Breakfast consisted of a ball of starch with brown sugar. Lunch consisted of bread made with the yeast of human urine and dinner was a soupy mixture of 100 grams of rice mixed with water and chopped white radish. Hannie was so malnourished that he could hardly walk. Deaths were common at the camp; an average of six people would die every day from countless diseases, dysentery and malnutrition.

The day before Christmas in 1944, one of his friends came up to him. "Hannie," he said excitedly, "Look what I have here, a cat!" Hannie followed him and behind the little house he saw that, indeed, his friend had caught a cat. They knew immediately where the cat came from. On the other side of the bamboo fence was the house of the Japanese camp commander and his concubine. The concubine's cat must have sneaked out of the house, crawled through the slokan (gutter), and ducked underneath the fence, where Hannie's friend grabbed it.

Without thinking twice, Hannie wrung its neck and skinned it with the help of a piece of barbed wire. Hannie and his brother came up with a brilliant idea. Because of Christmas, all prisoners had received a double portion of rice. Everybody pitched in and the news spread like wildfire through the camp: the Blaauw brothers have made nasi goreng (fried rice)! What a very special Christmas dinner it was. It was the highlight of Hannie's camp life.

For days thereafter, they could hear the camp commander's concubine call her cat-to no avail. Had they found out what happened to it, they would have killed the boys; the war would last another seven months. The cat never came back.

46

One of Hannie's fellow prisoners had a small radio. One day, he whispered to Hannie, "Hannie, come, listen! The Americans dropped a bomb on Hiroshima in Japan! Lots of dead Japs, man! Perhaps they will surrender."

But the Japanese did not give up that easily. For help they turned to Russia, with which they had a Non-aggression Pact for five years. However, the Pact had ended on August 6, 1945, and Russia refused help. The Allies dropped a second bomb, this time on Nagasaki, on August 9. Still the Japanese did not surrender. Why not? Researchers found out that Japan tested an atomic bomb of their own, which they had just finished, on one of their small islands in the north. It failed. Only then Emperor Hirohito announced, "Moreover, the enemy has begun to employ a new and most cruel bomb, the power of which to do damage is, indeed, incalculable, taking the toll of many innocent lives", referring to the atomic bombings of Hiroshima and Nagasaki that occurred days before. However, he never mentioned the Soviet invasion that had also begun a few days earlier. Finally, and most famously, he said: "However, it is according to the dictates of time and fate that We have resolved to pave the way for a grand peace for all the generations to come by enduring the unendurable and suffering what is insufferable."

Eighteen-year-old Hannie Blaauw and his fellow prisoners were unaware of all of this, but the tension in the camp grew. Finally, on August 15, 1945 the war was over, the gates of the camps were opened and the prisoners were free to leave. Hannie was liberated along with 10,000 other Dutch, French, Australian, British and American POWs. Many remained in the camp temporarily because they didn't know where to go or were waiting to reconnect with family members and relatives in other camps.

During the years that followed it was not safe to go anywhere because young freedom fighters, led by newly elected President Soekarno, started a bloody fight for their independence from the Dutch with weapons acquired from the Japanese. It would last almost two years and cost the lives of more than 20,000 innocent people. Japanese soldiers shipped in from Formosa were assigned to protect the prisoners who were still in the camps; the gates were open, but at night curfew was strictly enforced.

Adriaan, one of the military nurses in charge of treating Japanese soldiers in the small camp hospital in camp Tjikudapateuh, working with very limited supplies during the war, had witnessed the deaths of many fellow prisoners who could have been helped with better medication. But the Japanese never distributed the supplies sent to the camps by the Red Cross, and they bluntly refused actual visits by the International Committee of the Red Cross to inspect the camps or limited them to a brief conversation with the camp commander-they allowed absolutely no contact with the prisoners.

Lists of prisoners in other camps circulated among the inmates in Camp Tjimahi. Hannie found out that his mother was in camp Kramat in Batavia, and on another list he discovered to his great joy the name of his brother Adriaan in camp Tjikudapateuh in Bandung. Immediately he made plans to go visit him.

Very early in the morning, when the sun just rose above the horizon, Hannie left Camp Tjimahi, walking west in the direction of Bandung.

Through the sawahs (rice fields) Hannie walked, passing kampungs (small villages) along the way, as the sun burned down on his head and bare arms. His klètèks (wooden slippers with a goat-leather or rubber band across the toes and pieces of car tires under the heels) made a happy sound on the pavement: klètèk, klètèk, and his heart sang, 'I'm going to see Adriaan, *I'm going to see my brother!*' It was a long walk, but after about three hours he finally reached his destination and walked through the gates of camp Tjikudapateuh. Without too much trouble Hannie found the hospital, walked in and asked for Adriaan. With a broad smile on his face he embraced his brother when he walked in, totally surprised.

It was a tearful reunion–the four years of hardship, hunger and horrors had left indelible marks on the young men and after Adriaan had asked permission to take the rest of the day off they went outside, and talked for hours in the shade of a waringin (banyan tree). Time went by very quickly and they went to the camp kitchen to get something to eat. It wasn't much, a bowl of rice and a ladle of soup, but the soup had meat in it, and vegetables, and it was plenty after the camp rations the brothers were used to: the war was over!

Before they knew it, the sun was setting and they realized it was too late for Hannie to return to Tjimahi in time for curfew. "You can stay here," urged Adriaan, "come with me." Together they walked through the hospital to the operating room; Adriaan took a key from his pocket and opened the door.

"You can sleep right here, on the floor underneath the operating table. Sleep well, I will come and get you in the morning."

49

Hannie fell into a deep sleep, exhausted from the long walk and the happy reunion with his brother. He awoke with a shock when bright lights went on and a booming voice said, "I'll be damned! What have we here? Who are you? What are you doing here? Get out, get up!"

"I'm Hannie, Adriaan's brother," Hannie said. "I walked here yesterday from camp Tji-mahi to see my brother, and then it was too late to return to my camp before curfew, so Adriaan let me sleep here."

"All right then, but you gave me the scare of my life," said the surgeon, and Hannie walked out of the room and went in search of his brother.

In the early afternoon they said goodbye and Hannie left after they promised each other that soon they would find their mother in camp Kramat and leave Java together in search of a better future in Holland.

It was hot on the road back to Camp Tjimahi. Hannie walked at a steady pace, his feet starting to ache underneath the hard rubber straps of his klètèks. After an hour, knowing that he was not even half way, he was so thirsty that he decided to get something to drink at a warung (small open air café selling cold bottled drinks) in the next kampong (small village). He walked into the kampong, wondering if they would have anything to drink so soon after the war. Even a cup of water would be good though, and the thought of cool water made him smile.

Suddenly, a man blocked his path. "Go back to your camp," the man said urgently. "Go quickly, hurry! Lekas, lekas, because terrible things are about to happen." When Hannie looked up, the man was gone. *That must have been my guardian angel,* Hannie thought, and without another look at the warung in the distance he turned around, back to the road, and as fast as his legs could carry him he hurried, his klètèks making a nervous sound, faster and faster, back to Tjimahi.

The next day, the Bersiap (Indonesian term meaning 'get ready') started: the violent and chaotic fight for independence of the Indonesian extremists right after World War Two. Young freedom fighters roamed the countryside, brutally killing all people in sight. Hannie was safe behind the closed gates of Camp Tjimahi.

Fast forward. Hannie went to the Netherlands by way of Singapore. Several years later, he found his sweetheart, Nellie; they got married in 1958 and emigrated to the United States of America in 1961. They were blessed with a son and two daughters and made a good life for themselves in California, after the initial difficult years as penniless immigrants.

In 1997 they moved to Prescott. Hannie competed in the Prescott Senior Olympics every year, winning gold and silver; for many years he volunteered at Meals on Wheels together with Nellie. When Nellie passed away, Hannie, supported by his many friends, carried on, cooking his own meals, volunteering, playing tennis, and taking care of his little pup Scotty, his new companion. When Hannie was 86, his daughter decided he lived too far away from her, and in June of 2013, Hannie moved with Scotty to a town in the California desert.

After a week, he called enthusiastically: "Ronny! There are eight tennis courts close by, and two swimming pools!" Two weeks later: "Ronny, I have nobody to play with. I guess I have to wait for the snowbirds". He never complained, but set out to make new friends. He offered to volunteer at the local hospital, but they had no use for him. In October, he called and said, "Ronny! I joined the church choir, a very large choir!"

"You did?" I said, "I did not know you could sing."

"I can't," Hannie said, "I cannot even read notes, but they accepted me and I am singing along. Pretty soon we will start rehearsing for Christmas."

And make new friends he did! He discovered pickle ball and is now an enthusiastic player with many other seniors in his town. The latest thing he told me was that he had purchased a ukulele and is taking classes. But learning to read notes is one thing, learning to read chords and then produce sounds with your eighty-six-year-old fingers is something else. "You are my Sunshine" is difficult for him to learn, but his teacher says he is making good progress, and I bet that one day he will play it beautifully. An absolute favorite, which he plays when he feels lonely, is "Don't Fence Me In".

On April 1st of 2014 Hannie celebrated his 87th birthday. Life threw him many curve balls, but Hannie knew how to swing to get far; he never gave up hope, he reached out to others even when he had to start over in a strange new environment far away from his old friends. He lives his life one day at a time, grateful for what he has today, thankful to live in this beautiful country, knowing that God has a plan for him, a plan to prosper and not for harm, a plan to give him hope, a plan for his future.

His positive outlook on life is the secret to live to a ripe old age.

RONNY HERMAN DE JONG
Eluding Death

Sticking his bayonet through the gedèk (bamboo fence), the Japanese soldier aimed to kill me. He missed. A little girl with blond braids, I was only five years old in March of 1944. The bayonet sliced through the air over my head. "Mamma!" I cried.

"Ronny, come here!" cried Mamma

Dropping my flowers I scrambled across the slokan (ditch) and into Mamma's arms. "Oh Ron!" said Mamma. "I am so glad you could run so fast through the slokan! You're such a big girl!"

"What was that, Mamma?"

"You probably came too close to the gedèk. On the other side is a soldier. He thought you were running away and put a stick through the gedèk to scare you."

"Can you get my flowers, Mam? They are for you."

Mamma took my hand. "We will get them later, when the soldier is gone. All right?"

That morning, Mamma and I were walking along the edge of the camp. I was picking wildflowers for Mamma across the slokan. On the other side of the gedèk, a Japanese guard heard voices and intended to kill me. It is one of the bad memories I have of those three and a half years in Japanese concentration camps. At that time, Mamma, my little sister Paula and I were incarcerated in Halmahera, a Japanese concentration camp outside of Semarang, on the island of Java in the Dutch East Indies. The war had gone on for two years.

The Japanese Army had conquered our island in March of 1942. Civilians-men, women and children-were put into concentration camps. Our captors withheld food and medication and treated the prisoners in the most inhumane way. Many were tortured and raped and beheaded. The Imperial Japanese Army's instructions were to exterminate the Western Race in the islands at all costs so Japan could achieve a monopoly in Southeast Asia.

It was a near miss. I did not die at the hands of that Japanese soldier in 1944 because I was too small. I could have died a year later from hunger edema. In August of 1945, I was six. My legs were like sticks, my tummy was bloated and my cheeks were puffy. I was in the last stages of beri-beri, hunger edema. Paula, then four years old, had dry edema and was a mere skeleton. She could not walk or sit anymore. I imagined how it would happen. Paula would die first. Mamma had "wet" edema, like me, and she would die soon after Paula. I would have a month, perhaps two, before it was my turn. The Japanese would throw me into a mass grave outside the camp; a large hole in the ground dug especially for this purpose. When the war was over, allied rescue troops would unearth my body with all the others and bury it properly in the cemetery outside of town. They would top my grave with a nameless white cross. They put white crosses on thousands of graves in memory of the women and children who perished under the cruel treatment of the Japanese.

Forty-nine years later, I stood at that cemetery and wept. I wept tears of sorrow for all those mothers and children who had perished, and I wept tears of joy because I was alive.

I did not die in 1945 from hunger edema, because on August 15, 1945, the Japanese Empire abruptly surrendered and the war was over. With perseverance, great love for her little girls, faith in God, trust in the ultimate victory of the Allied Forces, and hope to be reunited with Fokko, our Pappa, Mamma kept the three of us alive for almost four years. During our time in captivity, she wrote letters to her parents in the Netherlands, which was occupied by Germany, in a thick, black diary. Initially she wrote how we little ones grew up, then how Fokko, our Pappa, had to leave when the Japanese army invaded our island, and then about all the things that happened to us during those grueling years under Japanese occupation. When the war was over in Europe as well as in Asia, we returned to the Netherlands for a six-month furlough and she gave the letter diary to her parents in Middelburg.

The world knows a lot about the war in Europe, the German occupation and the Holocaust. This book captures an aspect of WWII that is unknown to many: the torture and deaths that took place in civilian concentration camps all over Asia under Japanese occupation.

Excerpted from: *Rising from the Shadow of the Sun: A Story of Love, Survival and Joy.*

CORRIE DEN HOED
Childhood Memories

Corrie den Hoed, a childhood friend from Surabaya, lives in the Netherlands and enjoys spending time with her children and grandchildren. She visited my mother, Tante Netty and my sister Paula for many years. When she heard that Paula had been admitted to the hospital, dying of cancer, she went to see her. Corrie was the last person to see her alive; Paula died two days later. I will always regret that my little sister died alone; but she never told anyone about her cancer-she was firmly in charge of her own life; she did it her way.

A little girl of five, I felt very much alone in the world right after the war. I had lost my mother and her unborn baby just before I was incarcerated by the Japanese in a camp on the island of Sumatra. Her grave was washed away by a torrential flood; my father and I have never been able to locate it.

After the Japanese surrender my father, who had narrowly escaped torture by the extremists fighting for their independence, finally found me and we went to live in Surabaya where he became the district manager in the Darmo area. We became friends with the Herman family who lived close by. I loved Tante (aunt) Netty; she became a second mother to me. I loved to play with Ronny and Paula and we went to the same school. We all eventually ended up in the Netherlands; in 1998 Oom (uncle) Fokko died; then, unexpectedly, Paula died in April 2011 and Tante Netty in November 2011. She was almost 102 years old and until the end of her life she was always thankful, loving and hospitable. She saw the silver lining of every threatening cloud. Yet when Paula died she was inconsolable for months.

For me, Ronny's book "Rising from the Shadow of the Sun" is truly a Story of Love, Survival and Joy. Based on Tante Netty's camp diary, it fills in the gaps of my life in the camps as a toddler and has happy memories of the years thereafter. For you it may fill in the gaps of four years in WWII history when innocent women and children were incarcerated, tortured, raped and starved to death by a ruthless army of Japanese and it will tell you about women's strength in dire situations. Women survived because of the love for their children. Ronny's Memoir shows that it is possible to truly survive deprivation and misery and find joy in life.

EDWARD SOWMAN
Pearl Harbor Survivor

By far the oldest WW II survivor I have met here in Prescott is Edward Sowman, born on August 19, 1917 in Webb City, Missouri. The family eventually moved to Denver, Colorado where Ed grew up together with a younger brother and sister. His father was a coal miner who died in an accident when Ed was 6 years old. Life was difficult. Because jobs were hard to find during and after the years of the Great Depression Ed joined the Navy right out of high school when he was seventeen.

At the age of 97 Ed's mind is sharp and his memories of the Pacific battles he was in are vivid and emotional, although the names of the islands and the exact dates are sometimes slow to surface. Together, we relived the victories of World War Two, when he served on the heavy cruiser USS New Orleans and I was a little girl living life one day at a time waiting for the ultimate victory.

Below is Ed's story.

On December 7, 1941, when the Japanese attack on Pearl Harbor took place, I was 24 years old, a U.S. Navy Radioman 2nd class serving on the USS New Orleans. My ship and our sister ship USS San Francisco were moored in the harbor at the time for repairs to our engines. The New

Orleans had been to the US for an annual overhaul at Bremerton, Washington, but there were still repairs to be done.

I was on deck, standing in line for breakfast when I heard the call "all hands to your battle stations"! Immediately three other radiomen and I headed to our battle stations in the aft of the ship. One bomb dropped nearby, and we got all the shrapnel; I saw the Oklahoma turn on her side; I saw the West Virginia sink; I heard the Arizona blow up. It was terrible.

New Orleans was taking power and light from the dock but with yard power out during the attack, our men on deck had to fire at the Japanese attackers with rifles and pistols. The crew was forced to break the locks on the ammunition ready boxes as the keys couldn't be located, and because the ship got no more power from the dock, the guns had to be aimed and fired manually. The gunners topside were ducking machine gun bullets and shrapnel, with no ammunition other than the few shells in their ready boxes. The ammunition hoists did not have power, making it nearly impossible to get more ammunition topside to the gun crews. The 54 Lb shells had to be pulled up by ropes attached to their metal cases. Every man with no specific job at the moment formed ammunition lines to get the shells to the guns, which had to be fired manually. Some of our crew were injured when a fragmentation bomb exploded close by. Thank the good Lord our ship suffered no severe damage during the attack.

We stayed right where we were for another day and got partial repairs done on three of our four engines, then were ordered to convoy troops to Palmyra and Johnston Atoll.

We returned to San Francisco in January 1942 for engineering repairs and installation of new guns. We sailed again in February, escorting a troop convoy to Brisbane, Australia; from Australia we took a convoy to Noumea, New Caledonia and returned to Pearl to join Task Force 11 and finish up our repairs. Then we took a convoy up to Guadalcanal. We went back to Pearl, our place to get supplies, and then got orders to join a task force to the north of us. We sure crossed the Pacific many times.

New Orleans sailed on 28 May, to surprise the Japanese in the Battle of Midway. On 2 June, we rendezvoused with the Yorktown force, and two days later joined battle. Three of the four Japanese aircraft carriers were sunk by hits from our Air Force. The fourth carrier was found and wrecked later. We never saw a ship while we were in the battle of Midway but we saw lots of aircraft; we were constantly under attack. Midway lasted for three days; we saved the Yorktown and sank 4 carriers; that victory changed the out-come of the war. The Japanese gave up and turned around and went home and we did the same thing, we went back to Pearl.

Then we got involved in the first major battle in Guadalcanal. The Japanese had an aircraft landing place north of Guadalcanal and they were sending troops in small boats and we did some shore side bombing. We were told to team up with the task force and stop the Japanese warships coming down attempting to deliver food and supplies to Japanese forces on one of the islands.

We picked up a load of marines, a whole task force, to land them on the island. Before we put the marines ashore we spent 2 days firing on the beach to clean it up so they would have a better chance. We kept supporting the marines with shell fire to the beach and eventually we patrolled the eastern Solomons for a few months before sailing back to Pearl to replenish.

With four other cruisers and six destroyers we fought on the night of 30 November, engaging a Japanese destroyer-transport force. At midnight, we took a torpedo which detonated the ship's forward magazines and gasoline tanks, and blew off 150 feet of our bow. We lost 200 men that night. Two hundred men.

The severed bow, including Turret No. 1, swung around the port side and punched several holes in the length of New Orleans' hull before sinking and damaging the port inboard propeller at the stern. But we saved the ship, kept her afloat, and the next morning, under her own power, she entered the harbor of one of the minor islands where the marines were in charge and stayed there for eleven days, camouflaged from air attacks.

After eleven days we sailed, stern first to avoid sinking, to Sydney, Australia, arriving on Christmas Eve. In Sidney, they replaced the damaged propeller and other repairs were made including the installation of a temporary stub bow. On 7 March 1943, sailing backward the entire voyage, we left Sydney for Bremerton, Washington, where they had a bow waiting for us in dry dock and put it back on the ship.

I was not a part of that because I was transferred to a school in San Francisco. After the schooling was over I came back to Bremerton where she ship was seaworthy again and very shortly after that we took off again and headed for Pearl Harbor.

The war was still going on but had almost come to its conclusion. I was transferred off the ship and was made

Radioman Chief Petty Officer and transferred to new construction. I left the New Orleans and went to Philadelphia and on to the battleship Wisconsin, the very first radioman on board that ship. After a while I was made Warrant Officer and sent to the Island Repair Unit in Long Beach, where I spent the rest of the war.

When the war was over I went back to my wife, whom I had married in 1941, and we lived in Bountiful, Utah, south of Salt Lake City. I stayed in the reserves and trained every week; worked several jobs here and there until, by golly, the president called all the troops and the navy reserves and I was one of them. I worked at the Long Beach Naval Shipyard at Terminal Island in Long Beach and lived there for fifty years before coming to Prescott. I lost my wife eighteen years ago. She is buried at the military cemetery in San Diego. I will join her whenever the good Lord takes me.

I recently had a fall and wrecked both my knees and now use a walker and a scooter. But I am happy here in Prescott. And I am very proud to have served on the New Orleans, one of the top four most decorated ships of World War II with 17 battle stars for her war service.

JEANNETTE HERMAN-LOUWERSE
December 8, 1941 War—Closer to Home

On Mondays I always enjoy an exercise program on the radio at 5:45 a.m. When I switched on the radio on Monday, December 8, I heard the announcer say that after the exercise program the Dutch Governor-General would give a speech. I thought immediately, *that's it*. It really scared me. The Governor-General solemnly announced that Japanese air and naval forces had treacherously attacked the American naval base in Pearl Harbor during the early morning hours of December 7th, and the Dutch East Indies had declared war on Japan. Then they played our Dutch National Anthem, "Wilhelmus."

At first the unknown aspect of it frightened and depressed me. I didn't know what to expect. After a while I thought, Oh well, let's have it. Mother and Father Kees have had to suffer in the Netherlands. Finally it's our turn to be afraid. We've had it so good all this time. We've had plenty of food while you've had none. In a way it is satisfying to know that now we'll have to sacrifice too. Of course the children are foremost on my mind in case of an attack. I have no fear for myself. I can always quickly duck underneath something, but these two little ones have to be protected. I don't really know what a bombardment will actually be like, so I'd better not boast too loudly about my own lack of fear. The air raid protection exercises were not in vain after all.

That particular Monday was different. Neighbors, naval officers' wives, were crying, because their husbands were at sea. I thought of Jos Vermeulen, Fokko's best friend, who was away on a practice flight. Fokko called to remind me to get the house ready for blackout. Everyone was buying blue cloth, which is much stronger than paper, because all of a sudden everyone realized that we were at war and it looked like it could take a long time. I still had a roll of blue paper, but decided to buy material as well. I started in the bedrooms. I nailed blue cloth and paper in front of the small glass windows high up on the wall, blue paper against the ventilation holes underneath those small windows, and a piece of material against the wooden blinds of the large windows in the bedrooms. The last piece had to be removable during the day; otherwise the heat would be too oppressive. I worked throughout the afternoon, for I wanted to finish it before Fokko came home. He has to stand guard for 24 hours every three days as head of the Air Raid Protection Service. I am so grateful that he hasn't been called for duty yet. He is in a dangerous spot. The dockyards, offices and workshops, all part of the naval base, are prime targets in Soerabaja. When it comes to that, we'll hope for the best.

Fokko didn't like to close everything off with blue paper or cloth, like most people do, in order to be able to have the lights on. He thought it would be too hot. However, after a few evenings of huddling together with the newspaper beneath a 15-watt screened bulb, while occasional visitors couldn't see anything at all, I suggested to at least try it. We opened most of the windows and closed off the openings with blue cloth so we could have the lights on and read normally. It is still very hot, and you wouldn't believe the swarms of mosquitoes in here. We always rub our arms and legs with citronella oil, and have the *flitspuit*, the spraycan with insecticide, handy. The evenings are no fun, although better than before.

All that covering-up took about a week. In the mean time we thought about a hiding place. I wanted to hide under the table, but Fokko suggested the *goedang*, which is a walk-in closet next to the bathroom, away from the main house, along the verandah. If the house collapsed, we wouldn't get the whole roof on top of us. I emptied the *goedang* and put a large wooden crate in it with a little mattress for the children, and a suitcase with some medical supplies.

Every Saturday afternoon they tested the sirens. To make it less scary for the children I made funny faces each time. I also showed Ronny the nice bed I had made for her and Paula in the *goedang* and promised her she could get in there when the toet-toet would go. Yesterday morning at ten o'clock we had our first air raid alarm, and Ronny, who was outside, ran into the goedang and was already lying down with her thumb in her mouth when I came in with Paula, wrapped in a towel after her morning bath. I was very calm. There seemed nothing to be afraid of in broad daylight. It will be scarier at night. Kokki, the cook, continued her work in the kitchen, and *Baboe*, the maid, kept hanging the laundry on the line. I told them to join us in the *goedang* if they saw airplanes overhead. We did hear airplanes, but no shooting. Later, when everything was declared safe again, we heard that the planes had been our own, thank goodness, but hadn't been identified in time to prevent the alarm.

The war has been going on for two weeks now near Singapore, in the Philippines, and even on British Borneo. The Japs are getting closer. We don't know whether or not to expect them soon in Soerabaja, a very desirable location. They advised us not to move away. Besides, we don't have the money, and I don't want to be in the mountains where there are no pediatricians. We could take the two-hour walk to Jopie Esser's if we had to, but that road, although very well defended, is the main road into the country, and I doubt that it would be safe. I am alone one night out of three and really have to get used to it. Everything is pitch dark outside. Fokko works weekends and holidays too. He takes a gas mask and helmet to work and wants me to buy one too, but they are sold out. We anxiously read the news reports and just have to wait and see how all this will develop.

Excerpted from: *Rising from the Shadow of the Sun: A Story of Love, Survival and Joy.*

JACK C. HARPER

One of America's Youngest Warriors (Age 16)–
United States Navy..." I was awarded five battle
stars, all before my 18th birthday."

I met Jack Harper recently in his home in Prescott. He is an amazing veteran of World War Two in the Pacific, who served two terms in the U.S. Navy and later on enlisted in the U.S. Air Force for service during the Vietnam War. Jack was one of the five original members of the American Legion Post #6 Color and Honor Guard in Prescott, who performs military honors for families of deceased armed-forces veterans, and do flag-raisings and colors-postings at numerous schools. He was also involved with DARE (drug-alcohol abuse education) programs. Jack has two sons and three grandchildren. His wife Bobbie of 58 years passed away in 2009.

I was born in Long Beach, California, on 17 June 1927. When I was four years old, my parents moved from California to Arkansas. Today this seems to me a "Grapes of Wrath" in reverse. However, my dad lost his job in California and thought that he could find work in Arkansas. Unfortunately, this did not happen and our lives only became more difficult.

I had been going to school and working at various jobs, but the hours were too demanding, so I dropped out of school in early 1942 to work full-time in a furniture shop.

The age limit was 16. I told them that I was 16 and they accepted me. I worked there for a year.

On my 16th birthday, I asked my dad to sign the papers for me to join the Navy. He was happy to oblige. My mother cried for the next three years. Her dark hair turned to grey. On 28 June 1943, I was sworn into the Navy and sent to San Diego, California for boot camp. After completing boot camp, I went to the naval base at Coronado for amphibious training. Upon completion of the training, I was assigned to Standard Landing Craft Unit 4 as a machine gunner on LCMs. We went to Pearl Harbor in October 1943 where I had more training in landings and in gunnery practice.

I participated in the amphibious landings in the Gilberts, Marshalls, Marianas, Pelileu and Okinawa. Fortunately, I was never wounded, although we lost several of our boat crew members from the original group. Because of my age, I felt that God watched over me.

I very well remember the terrifying experiences I had during that period. The first was landing with the first wave in the Gilberts, the second was being stranded on Roi-Namur on 12 February 1944 when the Japanese bombed us; and finally, the nightly kamikaze raids at Okinawa. During the period from November 1943 until April 1945, I was awarded five battle stars, all before my 18th birthday. This can't be a record, but it's a pretty good average considering that I got the third one on my 17th birthday at Saipan. It was the biggest birthday party I ever had!

During that period I served on the LST-482, the USS *Belle Grove* (LSD-2), SS *Cape Georgia*, (a merchant ship–as a temporary boat crew), USS *Kenmore* (AKA-221), and the USS *San Diego* (CL-52). I received my first leave after returning from Okinawa. That is a long time to be away from home when you are so young.

I was discharged on 6 December 1945, enlisted in the Naval Reserve, finished high school, and requested active duty. By March, 1948, I hadn't heard from the Navy, so I re-enlisted in the regular Navy. Unfortunately, by that time I was the sole support of my mother and sister, so in May, 1949, I requested an early discharge.

I got out, but I wasn't happy. I really hadn't adapted to being a civilian yet, so I joined the Air Force Reserve and again requested active duty. Finally, in early 1951, I was called up and sent to Alexandria, Louisiana. That is where I met my future wife.

I was released from active duty in 1952 and returned to Phoenix, Arizona, where I went to work for the Mountain

States Telephone and Telegraph Company as a lineman. I held numerous assignments within the company and was Security Manager at the time of my retirement in 1982. I joined the Arizona Air National Guard and became a load master on four-engine transport aircraft. I also trained to be an aerial-refueling boom operator. During my time in the Guard I flew 3,000 hours to destinations such as Europe, South America and Alaska.

In 1966, we started flying regularly scheduled supply trips to Vietnam. Talk about a though schedule! We would depart Phoenix on Thursday, and 12 days and 100+ flying hours later we would return to our regular civilian job. One trip would consume all allowable flight hours for a month. It still seems strange to think about leaving Phoenix, going to places like Hawai'i, Wake Island, Japan, Okinawa, the Philippines and Vietnam, then report back to my civilian job all in less than two weeks!

I retired from the National Guard on 15 July 1973 at the rank of Master Sergeant. Many new and exciting things have happened to me, but none equal my military experiences. I feel very fortunate to have been a part of helping America retain her freedom which so many take for granted. Few know of the sacrifices that were made by men, women, and boys such as me.

JEANNETTE HERMAN-LOUWERSE
The Transport

The blow still came unexpectedly. One day, shortly after I had written the last entry in my diary on February 18, 1944, the Japanese, through the district leader, told us that we were to leave on a transport in two days. Many streets were deserted, as many women and children had already been transported out of the city. Still we had hoped, against our better judgment, we would be able to remain where we were. It was not to be. We were allowed one suitcase of limited size, and whatever else we could carry. With the exception of a few very dear mementos, it was important to take things that would last, such as a pair of sturdy shoes for each of us, practical clothes, and a couple of strong sheets that I could use for different purposes. They also told us, that bunch of liars, that we were allowed to fill one footlocker with items we wanted to keep, which they would store for us until the war was over. Everyone packed and left their most valuable possessions in footlockers, but never saw any of them after the war. Some women buried silver in their back yards, but they were easily discovered with metal detectors and never returned.

It was not easy to pack just one suitcase. I constantly had to put things aside because they didn't fit in any more. When I finally finished, shortly before our departure, they announced that the suitcases had to be one size smaller. It caused more panic on top of all the commotion. Where could we all get a smaller suitcase at such short notice? Miracle of miracles: I managed to borrow one, and then had to start sorting and packing all over again.

When we were married in 1937, we were handed a large Bible during the church ceremony. On the first page it had our names, wedding date and name of the town: Middelburg. We took it with us to our new homeland, and now I had to leave it behind. I could only take the little Bible, a present from Mother and Father Kees, with their names in it. The large one simply didn't fit in the small suitcase. I leafed through it one last time and it was as if I felt the presence of my little grandmother, telling me, "Do as I do, my child, read one page a day." I packed it in the large trunk, which they would keep for us until the war was over. I worked until the wee hours, selecting and repacking. Even the small backpacks of the girls were vital. They each had to carry some of their own things, little as they were. We had to leave so much behind.

Over the last couple of weeks I had re-read Fokko's letters one by one, and then destroyed them. That saddened me deeply. Because I didn't know what was going to happen to us, I thought it better to do away with them. And so, the next day, we left 44 Moesistreet. We had to assemble on a field early in the afternoon during the hottest part of the tropical day. We were allowed to sit on the ground, but there was no shade anywhere. Although we each had a large straw hat and something to drink, the wait, especially for the little ones, was not easy. Hour after hour went by. It became 4 o'clock, then 5 o'clock. We were still waiting. It was almost dark by the time a number of trucks appeared, supervised by armed Japanese soldiers. We climbed in. They drove us to the railroad station, where we boarded a waiting train. We each had a seat on the train, but it was hot and crowded, while armed native and Japanese soldiers stood or sat in the aisles. We were well guarded!

Twilight in the tropics is short, and soon it grew dark. Mosquitoes were buzzing around us. By the time it was 8 o'clock, the children were tired and thirsty. I had brought sandwiches and water. I was glad I had brought Paula's potty for the children, because the bathroom on the train was very dirty. Stars appeared in the sky. Later, I saw the moon. The mosquitoes buzzed as we just sat there, not moving. The children fell asleep, sitting up. I took Ronny on my lap for a while, so little Paula, three years old, could lie down. The moon climbed higher. It became midnight. Would this last all night? Finally, around 1 a.m., we heard rattling and puffing in the quiet train station, a sign that something was about to happen. The train pulled out of the station. We traveled all night and part of the next day before the train came to a stop. According to some of the women, we had arrived in Semarang, a city on the north shore of Java. Was it the end of our journey? What was to become of us?

Japanese soldiers ordered us out of the station and made us climb into waiting trucks; quite a hassle for those tired women and little children, all carrying their own luggage. When the trucks were loaded, we departed. We drove along country roads for hours. People whispered the camp must be a long way from the city. At last we saw in the distance a bamboo fence, called a *gedèk*, with a large open gate the full width of the road. When we got closer, the first thing visible inside the fence was a furious Jap, armed with a club, hitting nuns from the street. The nuns had probably noticed the approaching trucks, as did the other women and children in the background, and wanted to come to our aid. Having journeyed for more than 24 hours, tired and exhausted, we felt like crying. They shouted at us to get off the trucks and stand in line to be registered.

Excerpted from: *Rising from the Shadow of the Sun: A Story of Love, Survival and Joy.*

BENJAMIN CANDELARIA
Communications Expert

For more than ten years this lively, active but disabled veteran and I have been friends.

I met him when we stood in line at a downtown theatre in Prescott to go see a play. He was leaning on two crutches but there was nobody with him to assist him in any way. He looked like a veteran, so I asked him, "Are you a veteran?"
"Yes," he said.
"Of World War Two, in the Pacific?"
"Of World War Two in the Pacific, the Korean War and the Vietnam War" he replied.

He became an instant friend, and I still enjoy the stories he tells me of those years he served his country. Here is one such story.

I was born in Redlands, fifty miles east of Riverside in Southern California in 1925, four years before the great depression so I am a depression baby. We struggled and suffered like everybody else, no money, no jobs, no nothing. But my mom and dad tried their very best and that's what we did.

When in time I entered my junior year in high school and the war rumors were starting about the Pacific and then of course in 1941 the Japanese attacked Pearl Harbor. I graduated two years later and have been asked many times 'Were you drafted, or what made you enlist?' Well, to be honest, I never felt a surge of patriotism, but I just thought it was the thing to do. My country was at war and they needed us guys to go to the front lines and so I enlisted. Seventeen days after I graduated I joined the navy; I went to Los Angeles and raised my hand. I went to San Diego for boot camp and I don't know what happened but I was transferred to the marine corps and sent to Noumea in New Caledonia for Marine Combat training.

I was in communications all this time. From there I went to Guadalcanal, Kwajalein, up the slot to the Marianas campaign and that's where my combat came in. We watched the forces go in to Tinian from aboard ship and then when it was our time to go we landed on Guam and we invaded the island of Guam. War is never nice, war is hell, like everybody knows and I don't want to talk about it much. It went rather evenly for us and we remained on Guam when that invasion was completed. Subsequently the war ended when we were still on Guam.

One day, after the island had been "secured", but as we found out, islands are never secured, because they leave stranglers behind and, rookies that we were we didn't realize that. So one day, four or five of us buddies went souvenir hunting as we called it. We were coming down the side of this valley and across the way I saw a cave and through the hole in the cave I saw a weapon leaning against the wall. Oh, a souvenir!

I ran down, jumped into the cave, and saw that the weapon was a mortar, a Japanese knee mortar, one that you wrap around you knee instead of stick in the ground. What a fantastic souvenir! I grabbed it and then detected movement to my right, so I slowly turned around and saw a number of Japanese in the back of the cave, and one of them turned to face me with his weapon in his hand.

I jumped out of the cave and yelled "Japs" and my buddies pulled out their grenades and sealed them in there. It was a heart-in-my-throat experience for me and really shook me up.

On the way back to camp we ran across a marine lieutenant colonel with four or five of his men, who stopped us and asked "What do have you got there boy? Let me see it. Well, this is a fine weapon, one of the best ones I have seen." He gave it back to me and told me to turn it in when I got back to camp. So much for my Japanese souvenir!

We went home to Pearl Harbor to be processed and returned to San Francisco in April 1946 to be dismissed from the service. That took several months.

For me that ended the war. I went home and started college. But then, my dad, who was never ill, became sick and was bedridden for 10 months, so I had to go to work to earn money.

When dad could finally go back to work I decided to go into the Air Force. I joined just in time to see the Korean War come in and after that Vietnam. I always remained in communications, my highest enlisted rank was Chief Master Sergeant. I served my country for almost thirty years.

I worked for the Department of State in Washington for a few years and then at many postings overseas. I found a wife in my hometown who was a Registered Nurse and we were happily married for 43 years, until she contracted lung cancer. Of our four children, one daughter and one son followed in their mother's foot-steps and both became Registered Nurses. At the last count I had seven grand-children. My life has been blessed.

JEANNETTE HERMAN-LOUWERSE
More Illness and Death

One of the rumors going around was that we would all be put on a transport to the island of Borneo to work in the mines. It was only a rumor, yet the transport from Soe-rabaja to this prison camp had started as a rumor too. We literally lived a day at a time.

In January, for my 35th birthday, I got a little homemade calendar from the thirteen year old girl in our room. I assume her mother had some paper and pencils for her three daughters. The little calendar was divided into little squares for each day of the month. Every night, with the thought Thank God, another day has passed, I crossed out another day.

Something else that spread, other than disease and rumors, was a bed-bug plague. We inherited the bugs from the old men and their Singapore beds. We never had them in any of my previous houses, but now they were bothering everyone. One night, just before we had to turn off the lights, Ronny, who was sitting with her doll on our top bunk, said, "Mamma, there's a bug on my doll, and another one on the mosquito net!" I wanted to put one foot on the bottom bunk as usual to pull myself up to get closer to her but discovered that I couldn't. It was a strange sensation. The fluids in my legs had risen up to my knees and I couldn't climb on the bed anymore. I gave Ronny a rag, and told her to kill the bugs with it as best she could. "The bugs will stink when you

kill them Ronny, but it's better than if they would bite you."
She was a brave girl, didn't complain, but had a lot of bug
bites the following morning.

During the middle of 1945, we lived in a very small
world: the world of our bunk bed and our suitcase. We
knew nothing about the big world out there. None of us in
the camp knew anything about the course of the war.
Sometimes I thought of the first victories of the Americans at
Port Moresby and Guadalcanal. I had heard about them
with my own ears, but what had happened after that?

Oh, how much strength it would have given us to live
through those last excruciating months if we had only known
that the Allied Powers in some areas in the Pacific, and the
Americans in others, had driven back the Japanese step by
step! If we had known of the capture of the Gilbert Islands
in November of 1943, and that the capture of the Marshall
Islands in January of 1944 had followed the capture of
Midway in 1942. If we had only known that, in November of
1944, Japan was bombed for the first time from the Mariana
Islands, and on March 10, 1945 the center of Tokyo was
ablaze! If we had known that, on April 1, 1945, Okinawa was
captured, unfortunately causing the loss of many young lives,
we would have realized why we were left alone more often.

I used the hours at home to work on the girls' dresses and
to make a romper for myself out of an almost new robe of
Fokko's. It was painstaking work, since I had to do
everything by hand. In the meantime, Ronny enjoyed the
reading and writing lessons I gave her, and worked with her
little pencil on her slate. She wasn't perky anymore. None of
the children in camp were. Paula often didn't want to eat,
and she was getting weaker and weaker.

Another tragic death, the death of a minister's wife, saddened our little community. According to her roommates, she had given most of her own rations to her three small children, who were always hungry as was everyone else. It wasn't surprising, considering that a day's ration consisted of a ladle of starchy watery porridge twice daily and a flat scoop of rice with a ladle of watery soup with an occasional small piece of vegetable in it. A diet like that was unthinkable for a growing child, and often fatal. Many elderly people, and infants and toddlers, died. The minister's wife paid with her life for her understandable desire to feed her children a little more. She grew weaker and weaker herself and died from malnutrition. In order to stay alive we each had to consume our own portions. And so, for her too, the ox wagon rattled out of the gate, leaving three children behind. Most of the deaths went by unnoticed. By then I didn't get out of our house much—only, together with Ronny, for our trips to the kitchen after the bell and, "Block five, get your food." That was the highlight of the day: food!

Excerpted from: *Rising from the Shadow of the Sun: A Story of Love, Survival and Joy.*

THE NAVAJO CODE TALKERS
Unbreakable Codes

A very special group of Veterans distinguished themselves during World War II in the Pacific: the Navajos. During World War II, as the Japanese were breaking American codes as quickly as they could be devised, 29 Navajo Indian Marines provided their country with its only totally secure cryptogram. Recruited from the vast reaches of the Navajo Reservation in Arizona and New Mexico, from solitary and traditional lives, the young Navajo men who made up the Code Talkers were present at some of the Pacific Theatre's bloodiest battles. They spoke to each other in the Navajo language, relaying vital information between the front lines and headquarters. Their contribution was immeasurable, their bravery unquestionable. 420 Navajo Marine Code Talkers in total developed and implemented a communications system that proved unbreakable and helped to ensure the defeat of the Japanese and end the war in the Pacific. Many Code Talkers were killed in action and many were wounded, but their code remained unbroken.

After the war, they were all but forgotten and many ended their life in poverty. Not until 2001, 56 years after the war, did President Bush present four of the five original Code Talkers still alive-and relatives of the 24 others-with the Congressional Gold Medal at an afternoon ceremony in the Capitol rotunda. On Wednesday, November 20, 2013, Congressional leaders formally awarded the Congressional

Gold Medal to representatives of *all* Native Americans from 33 tribes for their service to the U.S. Armed Forces during World War I and World War II.

One of the last original 29 Code Talkers still alive was Chester Nez, living in Albuquerque, New Mexico. In 1943, 18 years old, Chester went off to war carrying medicinal herbs, a bearskin, corn pollen and arrowheads for good luck, all wrapped in deerskin. He was armed with a secret weapon as well: the Navajo language. He and 28 other young Navajos had been shipped to boot camp in San Diego, put in a big room and told to make a code in their own language that related to military terms, like planes, tanks, bullets. That took them almost 13 weeks.

The code, which they had to memorize, was based on a system in which the Navajo used their own words to substitute for the 26 letters in the English alphabet. What's more, the Navajo had no words applicable to modern warfare, so they settled on hundreds of descriptive words in their own language. A tank was a tortoise; a submarine, an iron fish; a dive bomber, a chicken hawk; a grenade, a potato; a battleship, a whale. Bombs were eggs, and the commanding general a war chief.

The week after the end of the war in the Pacific, August 15, the Navajo Nation celebrates National Navajo Code Talkers week in Window Rock, on the reservation.

I recently traveled to the Navajo reservation because I wanted to see the monument at the Navajo Code Talkers Veterans Memorial Park in Window Rock. A bronze statue–larger-than-life–of a Code Talker in full military gear, complete with radio, antenna and submachine gun is placed at the base of Window Rock, a mystical Redstone arch-shaped rock formation. The memorial park is shaped like a medicine wheel, to many Native Americans a primary representation of the four cardinal directions, the four sacred colors, the circle of life, and at the center the eternal fire. A circular path outlines the four directions; there are 16 angled steel pillars with the names of war veterans, and a healing sanctuary used for reflections and solitude with a fountain made of sandstone. It is a sacred place, like many areas on the Navajo reservation. It was a moving experience for me to look up at the huge bronze statue of the Code Talker and reflect on their gifts of life to many prisoners and troops alike.

Another impressive monument dedicated to the Code Talkers, installed in 1989 in Phoenix, Arizona, is an also larger-than-life bronze statue of a seated Navajo holding a flute. A plaque next to it states "Among many Native Americans, the flute is a communications tool used to signal the end of confrontation and the coming of peace."

I am eternally grateful to the heroic Navajo Code Talkers for their involvement in the Pacific war, which came to an end just before the Japanese Imperial Army would start to execute their order to "kill all prisoners in all POW camps beginning in September 1945".

JEANNETTE HERMAN-LOUWERSE
August 23, 1945

We did not look far into the future, and took life a day at a time, and no more. We were a tightly knit trinity. The little ones had only me and I had only them. We were not in very good shape at all as we sat on the porch steps, Paula between the two of us.

Suddenly, in the distance, I heard a deep, droning sound approaching rapidly. I recognized the sound of an airplane, looked up, and there, flying low over our heads, was a grey Catalina, a flying boat, a scout like Fokko used to fly in the Naval Air Force. Speechless, with wide-open eyes, I noticed on the wings the familiar round emblem: red, white and blue with the orange center. *Was this real?* In a split second the thought flashed through my mind: *Could it be the Japs up there? A trick? A captured plane?* Then, in the same second, after the initial total surprise, there was an explosion of excited voices all around us, crying, "That's our navy! Those are our men!" And then a mixture of exclamations, "Could the war be over? Could it be true?" We were afraid to believe it. We just couldn't believe it. It is indescribable what I felt. But there, after having veered to the left, the plane came back again. We waved and cried and then it was gone, leaving us behind with our emotions.

Excerpted from: *Rising from the Shadow of the Sun: A Story of Love, Survival and Joy.*

GUY WILLIS
My Navy Days 1945-46:1950-54

One of the youngest WW II veterans I have met in Prescott is Guy Willis. Born in Fayetteville, Tennessee in 1927, he graduated high school at Columbia Military Academy in 1945, after which he "immigrated" to Albuquerque, New Mexico where part of his family had moved while he was in school. Since he was still seventeen, he spent the summer working in Albuquerque loading and unloading planes for MATS (Military Air Transport Service) at the Kirtland Air Base, trying to decide not whether he would enlist, but which branch of the service to enter. Although the war was winding down, he decided to join the Navy. What was so interesting for me was the fact that he was living in Albuquerque, New Mexico when the first atomic bomb was tested at White Sands Missile Range: the first test of the bombs that would end the war in the Pacific and save my life; the beginning of the Atomic era. The local morning papers reported that the flash and sound, seen and heard by many, was the result of an ammunition depot blowing up.

Below is an excerpt of Guy's years in the US Navy starting with his First Enlistment, 8/1945.

As the summer waned and my 18th birthday approached, I enlisted in the Navy and was soon in boot camp in San Diego. When my draft got off the train we were greeted by salty seamen recruits, who preceded us by 6 or 8 weeks. Their warm welcome was memorable: "You'll be sorry!" While in boot camp the Hiroshima and Nagasaki "shots" took place. In my mind those were just two more tests, and I was anxious like everybody else for the war to be over.

Following Navy boot camp and two weeks of "boot leave" I reported to the Naval Receiving Station at Terminal Island, California, for 90 days of mess cooking, the least desirable task in the Navy. In late February I had completed my 90-day sentence and received orders to board USS *Chilton (APA38)*, my very first ship. Once aboard I was assigned to one of the deck divisions like all incoming seamen. I was a first class seaman, SN1, soon upgraded to the ship's mailman. For the ten or twelve days on the ship at Terminal Island I picked up the mail from the post office in one of the two jeeps that were on board, sorted and distributed it, sold stamps and so on. It was a really plush job.

The *Chilton* was an APA, which in Navy lingo translates to an Attack Transport. *Chilton* had participated in the Okinawa landings when she was hit by a kamikaze on April 2, 1945. During the war her purpose was to provide transportation for attack troops right up to the beaches. As a result the ship had numerous landing craft hanging all over it. Since we were in transition from "attack" to "troopship" we went to Long Beach Naval Shipyard, off-loaded a lot of our landing craft and then left for Pearl Harbor.

After a routine stay at Pearl Harbor we departed for Okinawa and arrived shortly before Easter of 1946. The beach was a shambles with high and dry landing craft, grounded ships and so on. I assumed this to be the result of the invasion just a year before but soon found out the damage resulted from a typhoon a few months earlier. We were anchored out, so several landing craft were promptly put into the water and "my" jeep was taken out of the hold and put into a LCM (Landing Craft Mortar). Mail pickup having a high priority, I was in the first boat to hit the beach and was one of the few enlisted men to get ashore at Okinawa since there was no liberty. The landing craft were busy bringing troops aboard. Nearly all were marines; many of them had not been "Stateside" for years so they were anxious to go home.

Having all the troops on board did cause the crew some inconvenience since the decks were crowded and there was always a chow line. When only the crew was on board the mess hall tables were down at normal height and we sat on benches. With the troops aboard, the tables were raised on their stanchions and the benches were removed, so we all had to stand at the tables to eat. This wasn't too bad while we were anchored, but at sea it got a bit difficult to remain stable against the ship's movement.

Once loaded we headed for San Francisco via the Great Circle. At sea my postal duties settled into routine except for the packaging and stamping of souvenirs to be mailed: Japanese rifles that a lot of the troops had brought aboard. By the time we reached port my little cubicle was getting a bit crowded.

Arrival in San Francisco was a joyous event I will never forget. We tied up on the south side of Pier 5, right downtown. The warehouse on the pier was decorated with banners; the open area was crowded with people, bands were playing on the dock and it was a real "Welcome home". I had only been gone for a few weeks but I can imagine how the Marines must have felt after being gone for a few years.

We left San Francisco and set sail for Long Beach Naval Shipyard, which was a beehive of activity. They were preparing for the fourth atomic bomb test at Bikini lagoon (followingTrinity, Hiroshima and Nagasaki). In preparation the battleship *Nevada* was being painted with red lead from stem to stern since she was to be the visual target for an aerial drop. There were numerous other ships being prepared for the test including the carrier *Saratoga*, one of the first US aircraft carriers, as well as several captured Japanese and German ships.

After a few days we departed for Pearl Harbor with no troops on board. During the Stateside stopover we did get a Third Class Mailman on board so I became a quartermaster striker. We maintained navigational charts, kept the log on the bridge and assisted the navigation officer with his responsibilities. At Pearl, a lot of target support ships were in port, in anticipation of the upcoming activity at Bikini, identified as "Operation Crossroads". From Pearl we went to the Marshall Islands; first to Kwajalein, where we anchored in the bay for a few days, then on to Eniwetok where we dropped the hook in the lagoon.

After 8 or 10 days in the lagoon we started loading passengers. It was a mixed bag of sailors, marines, army and everyone else. Once loaded we steamed out of the lagoon and headed for Majuro, now the capital of the Marshall Islands. Our objective was to get ourselves and the other people away from ABLE, which was a B-29-dropped A-Bomb scheduled for July 1. The caution was based on the fact that nobody knew what to expect of the bomb being tested and the function of our ship was to evacuate people just in case anything went awry. We were so far away from the blast however, that we neither saw nor heard anything and Eniwetok experienced no radiation or damage. A couple of days later we went back, discharged passengers and soon headed for Pearl.

It turned out that the bombardier of the B-29 who had dropped the ABLE bomb was so far off course that the bomb sunk a couple of ships on the outskirts of the fleet but only scorched the red paint of the *Nevada*. BAKER, the test in which the bomb was suspended below a barge and detonated 90 feet underwater, took place on July 25th while we were on the way back.

The trip from Pearl Harbor to San Francisco was uneventful. This was my first Navy experience. Back from the Pacific in August 1946 I was sent to Terminal Island to be discharged. I hitch hiked to Los Angeles and then along Route 66 back to Albuquerque to start my education at the University of New Mexico, where I met my future wife Dot.

As a result of the ABLE shot detonating so far from the target (USS *Nevada*) a program to improve accuracy of the drop was launched. A civilian with Sandia Corp in the late forties, I worked on this project. The drop site was Salton Sea in California. We, the drop monitoring crew, would fly there from Albuquerque early on Mondays in company planes, in order to be in place before the drops took place. Frequently, these early morning flights would result in a stop at Prescott, Arizona for breakfast. Throughout the remainder of the week dummy bombs were loaded on Air Force planes at Kirtland Air Base and flown over Salton Sea for the drops. To document the drop trajectory we were on the ground monitoring with movie cameras and telemetry systems.

Fast forward: In the summer of 1950 another war was underway and I enlisted in the service again, this time for four years. My second enlistment was from 1950 - 1954.

We recommissioned the destroyer USS *Walke* in San Diego on October 5, 1950 with CDR Marshall F. Thompson in command. After shakedown training along the west coast we departed on January 2, 1951 and set course for the Far East and service in the six-month old Korean War. Dotti and I were married just before I left, on December 30, 1950 and were happily married for almost 60 years.

During this second enlistment I had three tours of duty: USS *Walke* (DD723) until June 1951, when she was steaming some 60 miles off the Korean coast and got hit by a floating mine, which caused extensive damage, killing 26 men and injuring 40; NAVY SPECIAL WEAPONS UNIT 802 at Sandia Base, New Mexico; SS *Granville Hall* (YAG40), a target ship at Bikini tests.

I have many more stories to tell–this is just one of them.

ABOUT THE AUTHOR

Ronny Herman de Jong, born and raised on the island of Java in the Dutch East Indies, survived four years in Japanese concentration camps during World War Two. A B.A. in English Literature from Leiden University in the Netherlands served her well during the rest of her life after the war, since she immigrated to the United States in 1972 with her husband, three children and their dog. Her mother's secret camp journal was the basis for her first book *In the Shadow of the Sun*, published in 1992 and her memoir *Rising from the Shadow of the Sun: A Story of Love, Survival and Joy*, a five-star book on Amazon, published in 2011. Ronny currently resides in Arizona where she is a member of SSA, the Society of Southwestern Authors and PWP, the Professional Writers of Prescott. She has been interviewed on local Radio and Television shows and on SBS Dutch Radio in Australia. Her favorite things are traveling, reading, writing, walking, swimming and snorkeling. Her family, counting seven grandchildren, always comes first.

Ronny's website: www.ronnyhermandejong.com
Ronny's memoir: *Rising from the Shadow of the Sun: A Story of Love, Survival and Joy.*